PLACE, PERSONALITY AND THE IRISH WRITER

PLACE, PERSONALITY AND THE IRISH WRITER

edited by
ANDREW CARPENTER

Irish Literary Studies I

COLIN SMYTHE
GERRARDS CROSS 1977

First published in 1977 by Colin Smythe Limited
Gerrards Cross, Buckinghamshire

ISBN: 0–901072–63–X

Acknowledgements are due to Michael and Anne Yeats, to
Macmillan & Co. Ltd., London and Basingstoke, and the Macmillan Publishing Co., Inc., New York, for permission to quote
from the writings of W. B. Yeats, to the A.E. Estate for permission
to quote from the works of A.E., and to Dolmen Press Ltd., Dublin,
for permission to quote from the poems of Denis Devlin.

Produced in Great Britain
Set by Watford Typesetters Ltd., and
printed and bound by Billing & Sons Ltd.,
Guildford, London & Worcester

Contents

FOREWORD

The essays in this book were presented to the third triennial conference of the International Association for the Study of Anglo-Irish Literature, held in Galway in July 1976. The theme of the conference, chosen by Professor Lorna Reynolds, the inspired organizer of the week's activities, was 'Space, Place and Personality, and the Irish writer.' For this volume, I have altered the title slightly as, in the event, those who gave lectures concerned themselves more with place and personality than with the concept of space.

While most of the lectures were concerned with particular writers or areas of study, two were designed to be of a more general nature: the first in this book, which was intended to be the keynote speech of the conference, and the last which was intended to be its parting salvo. Apart from Richard Wall's paper, which was one of those tabled at the conference, all the papers were delivered as lectures.

It is intended that this volume should be the first of a series which will appear under the general title of *Irish Literary Studies*. It is hoped that the title will prove sufficiently wide for the series to include all kinds of scholarly work on Irish and Anglo-Irish literature. A second volume will appear later in 1977, and thereafter volumes should appear at the rate of at least one a year.

On behalf of IASAIL, I should like to thank all those who have contributed to this volume. I hope that many more such volumes will come from conferences on Irish and Anglo-Irish literature.

Andrew Carpenter.
University College, Dublin.

INTRODUCTION

LORNA REYNOLDS

In choosing the theme of 'Place, Space and Personality and the Irish Writer' for the 1976 Conference of IASAIL in Galway, I was influenced by the fact that so many of the writers of the Irish Renaissance had either come from the west of Ireland or had been regular visitors there. Ireland as a whole is a land of winds and of clouds in constant movement across the sky, thinning, dissolving, re-forming and thickening, playing with the light, in combination with it putting on sudden displays of aerial splendour, or in opposition casting sudden shadows and glooms on the earth. In the west, because of the extent of bogland and the nearness of the expanse of Atlantic waters, and the reflection therefrom thrown into the sky, the commerce between earth and sky, between light and shade, seems to operate on an even more splendid and more dramatic scale than elsewhere in the country.

It seems to me that nobody of any impressionability can escape being affected by this, and that the imagination must be drawn to the possibility of invisible agents behind the visible phenomena, to a realisation of the wildness and remoteness of this part of Ireland as recently as even the beginning of the nineteenth century, must be lifted and stretched by the vast reaches of space suggested by the characteristics of such scenes, must be lifted and stretched out of the present into a sense of the indivisibility of past and present.

Place therefore, as making the dramatic seem natural, and space as suggesting a continuum of time, is what I had in mind in choosing the theme for the Galway conference. I also thought of the concept of space as approaching somewhat Yeats's 'phantasmagoria', as the psychological backdrop of the writers, what each carried by tradition, by acquisition, by temperament in the way of the normal baggage of his mind. By personality I meant two things, the effect of space and place on the personality of the individual writer and the manner in which he was haunted by particular personalities such as Parnell, and how he dealt imaginatively with such hauntings.

In the event, what we got was, of course, different from what I had in mind: what we got was much more concrete than anything I had envisaged – and all the more valuable for that. Our contributors, having been stirred into thought by the theme, treated it in selective and idiosyncratic fashion. The result, we hope our readers will agree, is the casting of new light on some aspects of Anglo-Irish writing.

PLACE, SPACE AND PERSONALITY AND THE IRISH WRITER

A. NORMAN JEFFARES

We are all, I suppose, conscious of an impulse to discover the nature of the distinctiveness of Anglo-Irish literature. Where, we ask, is it different from English or Scottish literature, from Welsh or American literature, from Canadian, Australian, New Zealand, Indian, African or Asian writing in English? Is it distinctive because it is written by Irish men and women, or because it is written in Ireland, or about Ireland?

Even if we admit – as I think we must – that the place of Ireland is not all that distinguishes Anglo-Irish writing from other writing in English, yet we must also be aware of the fact that the physical entity of Ireland is an integral part of the atmosphere of much Anglo-Irish writing. I am inclined to believe that, as critics, we have paid too little attention to the importance of place in Anglo-Irish writing: in this paper, therefore, I want to look at the way in which some Anglo-Irish writers have dealt with the physical entity of Ireland: with its hills and plains, its rivers, loughs and seashore; with the place in which and from which, as Anglo-Irish writers, they have their being.

Sometimes, of course, Anglo-Irish writers see the scenery around them in much the same way as did others of their epoch who happened to be working elsewhere: sometimes, they bring in new attitudes which reflect their own interests and natures in a more personal way: sometimes they are of their age in some respects, while in others they are more original in their attitudes. I have chosen authors who span the period from the seventeenth century to the twentieth in order to compass some of the changes to be noticed in the way authors have seen and reported on Irish space in general, and on places in particular, revealing to the reader in the process not a little of their own personalities.

Where should we begin but with Swift? His attitudes to Ireland

11

are complex: his voyages from the larger island to the smaller –
where he happened, as he said, 'to be dropt' – do not seem to have
been made with pleasure. The only time he seems to have wanted
to get to Ireland quickly was when Stella was reported to be dying
in Dublin, and he was stuck at Holyhead for want of a favourable
wind:

> I never was in hast before
> To reach that slavish hateful shore
> Before, I always found the wind
> To me was most malicious kind
> But now, the danger of a friend
> On whom my fears and hopes depend
> Absent from whom all Clymes are curst
> With whom I'm happy in the worst
> With rage impatient makes me wait
> A passage to the land I hate . . . .[1]

The land, here, was the 'slavish hateful state', the body politic,
torn between religion and politics, economically miserable, not
doing what it could to help itself and therefore the more likely to
be more unfairly treated by its powerful, wealthy neighbour. But
what of the physical appearance of the place, in Swift's eyes? Here,
he seems to have been influenced by his education, his reading and
the general attitudes of the age. He was not any admirer of the
wilder aspects of the scenery. On one occasion, at a time of great
personal grief, he travelled to County Cork. It was immediately
after Vanessa's death in June 1723; he had broken with her in
April – probably because she had written to Stella about him and
Stella had given the letter to Swift – and he left Dublin the day
before her funeral. As his friend Dr Delany put it, he made a tour
to the south of Ireland 'to dissipate his thoughts and to give place
to obloquy.' This was probably the one time his relations with
Stella were estranged: she retired with Rebecca Dingley to Charles
Ford's house at Woodpark for six months.

When in Cork, Swift wrote his poem on Carberry Rocks: and he
wrote it in Latin. Perhaps he turned to Latin at a time of despair,
as Milton had turned to it when writing about girls in the spring,
but this poem's treatment of the scenery certainly shows no delight
in what it describes. '*Carberiae Rupes in Comitatu* Corgagensi *apud*

Hybernicos' stresses the dissonance, the dreadful murmur of the seas dashing upon the rocks: here is no appreciation of the sublime beauties of nature, no delight in wild and savage scenery for its own sake; the whole poem reminds one of early British travellers' attitudes to the Alps, which they saw as horrid and bristling, as barriers imposed by fierce Nature, as a hindrance to the traveller seeking the warmth of sunnier, kinder Italy.

No, Swift was of his age: no doubt he approved of the achievement of another Anglo-Irish writer, Sir John Denham, whose poem 'Cooper's Hill', described by Dryden as ever to be 'the exact standard of good writing', had established the *genre* or 'kind' of the local poem. Swift made his own poem 'Drapier's Hill' a deliberate literary echo, while adding his own ingredient of irony:

> We give the World to understand
> Our thriving Dean has purchas'd Land.

This action might, he comments, preserve his fame when the nation 'long enslav'd, Forgets by whom it once was sav'd' and when

> His famous LETTERS made waste Paper;
> This Hill may keep the Name of DRAPIER;
> In Spight of Envy flourish still,
> And DRAPIER's vye with COOPER's Hill.[2]

But a later poem gives us perhaps even more of the intrusion of Swift's own attitude in this kind of poetry. In 'The Dean's Reasons for not Building at Drapier's Hill', he describes how Gosford's knight does not seem to entertain any of the orthodox country pleasures – visiting, riding, walking, hunting, fowling, playing cards, dice or bowls. He writes (in a way that reminds one somewhat of Milliken's later 'Groves of Blarney') in a deliberately bucolic style, as he describes how the knight,

> . . . Seated in an easy chair,
> Despises exercise and air.
> His rural walk he ne'er adorns;
> Here poor Pomona sits on thorns:
> And there neglected Flora settles
> Her bum upon a bed of nettles.[3]

Nature to be enjoyed needed to be nature methodis'd, and Swift did enjoy methodising it. Some of the pleasantest references in the *Journal to Stella* are those dealing with his garden at Laracor in County Meath. From London he enquires anxiously of the ladies in Dublin about the state of the holly, cherry, apple and willow trees he has planted, of the canal he has dug. He is worried lest the apple trees which he has taken such care to plant in a sheltered place be blasted; he wishes to be back, away from London and the Court, and he indulges himself in memories of the journeys from Dublin to Laracor, and of his eel and trout fishing there. Indeed, one passage has a lyrical, rhapsodical quality about it.

> Oh, that we were at Laracor this fine day! the willows begin to peep, and the quicks to bud. My dream's out: I was a-dreamed last night that I eat ripe cherries. – And now they begin to catch the pikes, and will shortly the trouts (pox on these ministers), and I would fain know whether the floods were ever so high as to get over the holly bank or the river walk; if so, then all my pikes are gone; but I hope not. Why don't you ask Parvisol these things, Sirrahs? And then my canal, and trouts, and whether the bottom be fine and clear?[4]

Obviously Swift had enjoyed making Laracor viable; he had enjoyed wandering in the garden in his dressing gown; he liked air and exercise and it provided both; and even when he was appointed to the Deanery, he thought Laracor would have to provide what he had to live on. Laracor was, however, in part a literary activity, in that it was his Sabine farm. He saw the parallels between court life and country life in Horatian terms: for 'fig and wine' read 'apple and cherry', and with them read the economic pleasures of producing your own methodised fruit.

To move from Swift to Goldsmith is to keep within the ambit of a literary, classically inspired pastoral tradition. Goldsmith, for instance, gave us in *The Vicar of Wakefield* a beautiful piece of scaled-down pastoral in prose where the continuity of simple country life is skilfully compressed into a couple of paragraphs. His picture of a village, in 'The Deserted Village', appears to be a generalised picture such as would meet eighteenth-century taste – no painting the streaks of the tulip – though the basis for his village was probably – no, surely – Lissoy near Ballymahon.

14

The sheltered cot, the cultivated farm,
The never-failing brook, the busy mill,
The decent church that topped the neighbouring hill,
The hawthorn bush, with seats beneath the shade,
For talking age and whispering lovers made.[5]

(ll. 10–14)

The editor of the 1833 edition of Goldsmith's *Miscellaneous Works* remarked drily that Lissoy had become the fashionable resort of poetical pilgrims, and had paid the customary penalty by furnishing relics for the curious. 'The *hawthorn bush* has been converted into snuffboxes,' he wrote, 'and now adorns the cabinets of poetical virtuosi.' Just as this bush was used for souvenirs, so the poem's scenery was used for a background to the full, happy, continuous life of the village; then, later, in different vein, for a background to the desolation of depopulation.

No more thy glassy brook reflects the day,
But, choked with sedges, works its weedy way.
Along thy glades, a solitary guest,
The hollow-sounding bittern guards its nest;
Amid thy desert walks the lapwing flies,
And tires their echoes with unvaried cries.
Sunk are thy bowers in shapeless ruin all,
And the long grass o'ertops the mouldering wall. . . .

(ll. 41–48)

The poem centres upon the population's departure, and the poet describes his imagined return:

Here as I take my solitary rounds,
Amidst thy tangling walks and ruined grounds,
And, many a year elapsed, return to view
Where once the cottage stood, the hawthorn grew . . . .

(ll. 77–80)

This leads him to the poignant paragraph which seems pure Goldsmithian autobiography (for it chimes with those letters he wrote back to Bob Bryanston and his own family – to which he seems to have had no reply): in all his wanderings and griefs, he says,

15

I still had hopes my latest hours to crown,
Amidst these humble bowers to lay me down;
To husband out life's taper at the close,
And keep the flame from wasting by repose.
I still had hopes, for pride attends us still,
Amidst the swains to show my book-learned skill,
Around my fire an evening group to draw,
And tell of all I felt, and all I saw;
And, as a hare, when hounds and horns pursue,
Pants to the place from whence at first she flew,
I still had hopes, my long vexations past,
Here to return – and die at home at last.

(ll.85–96)

Again the emphasis is on the social reality: the place is important, but the place from whence the hare flew is important because of the company there which would understand him. His memories continue with memories of the sounds:

The swain responsive as the milkmaid sung,
The sober herd that low'd to meet their young;
The noisy geese that gabbled o'er the pool,
The playful children just let loose from school . . . .

(ll.117–120)

The present sights – garden flowers grown wild, torn shrubs – remind him of the village preacher, while the straggling fence now 'With blossomed furze unprofitably gay', recalls the village school-master, and the thorn, which has replaced the sign-post, recreates memories of the village statesmen in the inn. The emigrant villagers are in new surroundings:

Those matted woods where birds forget to sing,
But silent bats in drowsy clusters cling.

(ll.349–350)

They measure their inhospitable savagery by the old and mild pastoral scenery:

The breezy covert of the warbling grove,
That only sheltered thefts of harmless love.

(ll.361–3)

One of Goldsmith's friends in London was Bishop Percy, after whom *Percy's Reliques* are named; his spirit of antiquarianism symbolised a fresh turn in English eighteenth-century intellectual attitudes – one thinks of Gray, Chatterton and the Wartons – and this tide of antiquarianism flowed through Ireland a little later. It profoundly affected literary ideas about places, for patriotism naturally tends to emphasise place, which, however far back into the past patriotism penetrates, is always there. The first example of an increasing Irish interest in the past came with Sylvester O'Halloran's *General History of Ireland* (1774). This interest in history spread to a broader view of culture during the euphoria created by Grattan's apparent political settlement in 1782. Joseph Cooper Walker's *Historical Memories of the Irish Bards* (1786) was followed by Charlotte Brooke's *Reliques of Irish Poetry* (1789), and these two volumes were subsequently complemented by Edward Bunting's three collections of the *Ancient Music of Ireland* (1796, 1809 and 1840).

The movement of Irish thought in the last three decades of the eighteenth century, then, was away from classicism into antiquarianism and patriotic romanticism, and in the process, the landscape achieved its new importance. If we look at the early novelists, for instance, we see the older classical attitudes prevailing in Maria Edgeworth. Her comment on her father's move to Ireland in 1782 stresses his awareness that 'till his own home was comfortable, he could not pursue his principal objects; he could not get any example of neatness and order, or of propriety and proportion in his mode of living.'[6] Doomed to a place, she went on, where 'nothing sublime or beautiful could be found' he contented himself that time and industry might make the whole estate of Edgeworthstown 'neat and cheerful.'[7] Pakenham Hall was twelve miles away and 'there was a vast Serbonian bog between us; with a bad road, an awkward ferry, and a country so frightful, and so overrun with yellow weeds, that it was aptly called by Mrs Greville "the yellow dwarf's county." '[8] Her father's attitude to bogs was the practical, utilitarian one: that they should be drained. When he was 65, he took charge of 34,500 acres of bogland and reported to the Commissioners in 1810 that the improvement of this 'vast tract of bog was not only practicable but would prove highly profitable.'[9]

Maria's descriptions of nature were also practical. Her account of how the family returned to Edgeworthstown after their

17

dangerous situation in Longford in the summer of 1798 is one of the few where she permits herself the vestige of an enthusiastic, emotional response to nature, and even this reaction is firmly based upon an economic attitude – the *triste utilité* of which Madame de Staël had accused her:

> The joy of having my father in safety remained, and gratitude to Heaven for his preservation. These feelings spread inexpressible pleasure over what seemed to be a new sense of existence. Even the most common things appeared delightful; the green lawn, the still groves, the birds singing, the fresh air, all external nature, and all the goods and conveniences of life, seemed to have wonderfully increased in value, from the fear into which we had been put of losing them irrecoverably.[10]

Sydney Owenson, later Lady Morgan, looked at the landscape – notably that of the west – with a very different attitude indeed, for she saw the countryside through painters' eyes, searching for the picturesque, while accepting at times some misty Ossianic blurring of the edges. The glowing fancy of Claude Lorraine, she remarked, would have dwelt enraptured on the paradisial charms of English landscape; she, however, was stirred by what she considered the superior genius of Salvator Rosa, who inspired her most emotional descriptions. Her novels echoed the imagery of his paintings and she wrote an enthusiastic book about him in 1824. She liked his 'wild and gloomy imagination'; but while she admired his work with an enthusiasm 'unknown perhaps to the sobriety of professional virtu,' she estimated his patriotism still more highly. This, she thought, had led him to step boldly in advance of a degraded age when all around him was 'timid mannerism and grovelling subserviency.'[11] If Claude of Lorraine would have delighted in the 'paradisial charms' of English landscape then, according to the hero of her novel *The Wild Irish Girl* (1805), the 'superior genius of Salvator Rosa would have reposed its eagle wing amid those scenes of mysterious sublimity with which the wildly magnificent landscape of Ireland abounds.'[12]

Her patriotism was based, in part, upon the antiquarian movement's discoveries about the past: the existence of a Gaelic civilization. In part she came to this through her interest in music, for she sang and played the harp; in fact, in 1805, she published a volume of *Twelve Original Hibernian Melodies*. In her third novel, *The Wild Irish Girl*, she introduced Ireland's present plight in contrast to its past glories. She equipped her ancient Irish chieftain with an Irish harper, in addition to his chaplain, his Gaelic manuscripts, his druidical cromlech and his ruined castle – destroyed, of course, by the Cromwellians. The heroine, the chieftain's granddaughter Glorvina, like Sydney herself, also played the harp. This enthusiastically romantic, yet pedestrianly pedantic, novel was also Ossianic and Gothic. Its plot (borrowed, perhaps, in Maria Edgeworth's *Ennui* of 1809 and *The Absentee* of 1812) introduced a stranger into Irish life – particularly into the very different life of the west. The novel's hero, Mortimer, *en route* for the steep Atlantic shores of North Connaught, remarked on the bold features of the varying landscape, on

> the stupendous attitude of its 'cloud-capt' mountains, the impervious gloom of its deep-embosomed glens, the savage desolation of its uncultivated heaths and boundless bogs, with those rich veins of à picturesque champagne, thrown at intervals into gay expansion by the hand of nature. . . .[13]

The young man described Connaught as containing the character, the manner, the language and the music of the ancient Irish in all their primitive originality. And all this is set in landscape 'diversified and enriched' by groves druidically venerable – mountains of Alpine elevation – expansive lakes, and 'the boldest and most romantic sea coast.'[14] Every feature finely combined either the beautiful or the sublime. Small wonder the hero and heroine develop intensely romantic sensibility, not to say sentimentality, under the influence of such emotive scenery.

Maturin, however, while he cashed in on the popularity of one of Lady Morgan's titles, even using for one of his novels the title *The Wild Irish Boy*, had a very different attitude to scenery. For him it had Wordsworthian pick-me-up effects and he blends a mixture of Wordsworthianism and a Rousseau-istic return to nature with his own brand of nationalism. His first novel *Fatal Revenge; or, the Family of Montorio* (1807) went beyond Scott's poetry and Irish ballads to the *Lyrical Ballads*, which is the real foundation of his romantic nationalism – Irish resistance to English rule being part of a clash of cultures, the English neoclassical and cosmopolitan, the Irish relying on a Gaelic folk tradition and living in close contact with nature. This was an entirely new idea in Anglo-Irish writing. *The Wild Irish Boy* (1808), though it is but a pot-boiler, shows the effect of three years spent in the lake district on Ormsby Bethel, the wild Irish boy, who thinks of this period as a species of romantic intoxication.

Maturin did better in *The Milesian Chief*, where he also used nature as a backdrop. When Wandesforth the English officer travelled across Connaught, the elements as well as the inhabitants were hostile:

> The sun set: the country was one bleak expanse of snow, intersected by tracts of bog to which the unfrozen water gave a dusky hue; the sky livid and lowering with the pallid gloom of winter, seemed to denounce all its terrors against the travellers.[15]

And the desolation of the heroine, Armida Fitzalban, was heightened as she too travelled to the west across a bleak waste of bog, 'scarce seen through the rain that beat heavily against the carriage windows.' Indeed 'she shuddered at the thought of becoming the inhabitant of such a country; and she thought she felt already the wild transforming effects of its scenery.'[16] She fell in love, promptly, unsuitably, and unhappily – she, the daughter of the civilized world – with Connal, the offspring of a wild romantic ancient race. She liked Italy and Italian scenery; but, despite never having been there, he, in his proud patriotism, completely and utterly despised it: no scenery could be as good as Ireland's. It certainly served, in this novel, to heighten the air of tragic doom-laden despair as rain and storms swept across ruins, solitary islands, bogs and barren mountains. This emphasis on wastes of dreariness may remind us that Maturin had disliked being a curate in Loughrea. Though he enjoyed staying in the O'Moore's Castle at Cloghan where he found ample copy for *The Milesian Chief*, the poverty of the flat lands west of the Shannon displeased him and in the words of the *Irish Quarterly Review*, 'he worked anxiously and continuously to obtain a curacy in some other locality where he would occasionally at least, see other things beside "priests, pigs and peelers" who, Henry Lorrequer tells us, "form the chief objects of interest and for whom there seems to be an insatiable demand in the neighbourhood of Loughrea." '[17]

Maturin, however, could write in lighter mood, and *Women*, the first study of an undergraduate's love affair, as well as being perhaps the first piece of urban gothic, relies on a different kind of scenery for its effects. In this novel he was writing of the places in which he himself had grown up, Dublin and Wicklow. This scenery, less a product of Salvator Rosa and Lady Morgan than was the west of Ireland in his other novels, seemed suitably Wordsworthian in its effects: Killiney, for instance, produced tranquillity.

Beneath them, to right and left, lay the bays of Dublin and Killina, still as if in the first moment of their creation, before they had felt the rush of the breeze, or the ripple of the tide. The low murmur of the waves, that scarce reached their ears, seemed to send a voice of deep, lonely tranquillity to the heart, where its tones were addressed. It seemed to say – 'Listen to us and be at peace'. The grey hill, smooth to its summit, the rude obelisk against which they leaned, and which appeared rather like a thing placed there by Nature than by man, all around them seemed to mark the boundary between the world of Nature and of man. They felt themselves alone, and they felt, what those who live alone can feel, that such moments of abstraction are moments of the most exquisite enjoyment.[18]

There is a delightful equestrian picnic in this novel where the main characters explore the wild, mountainous scenery of Lugge-law in County Wicklow. This picnic was arranged by Zaira, the blue-stocking opera singer, who exposed the 'theology of the heart' in her raptures over the beauty of nature. Intellectually tough, Zaira, unlike the other heroine Eva, was not at all terrified by a sudden thunderstorm; 'Quite a female Plato', in the eyes of a northern Irish Trinity College student, she lectured away, as if on the promontory of Sunium, amid the lightening flashes of a summer storm. But this storm, which built up the novel's tense mystery, discharged its function once a mad old woman had uttered her sinister warnings, and

the clouds, rising slowly above the Killina hills, soon spread far south; Bray-Head was enveloped from its summit to its base; and the long sweeping folds of leaden-coloured vapour passed from hill to hill southward, like giant spectres gliding over their sum-

21

mits, and leaving the folds of their mysterious mantles lingering and darkening on the track of their progress.[19]

Though Maturin was steeped in Wordsworthian ideas about nature, his penchant for the Gothic kept breaking out; and in *Melmoth the Wanderer* he used an eerie description of a country house in Wicklow to set the tone for the Gothic horrors which follow – and follow:

> The weather was cold and gloomy; heavy clouds betokened a long and dreary continuance of autumnal rains; cloud after cloud came sweeping on like the dark banners of an approaching host, whose march is for desolation. As Melmoth leaned against the window, whose dismantled frame, and pierced and shattered panes, shook with every gust of wind, his eye encountered nothing but that most cheerless of all prospects, a miser's garden – walls broken down, grass-grown walks whose grass was not even green, dwarfish, doddered, leafless trees, and a luxuriant crop of nettles and weeds rearing their unlovely heads where there had once been flowers, all waving and bending in capricious and unsightly forms, as the wind sighed over them. It was the verdure of the church-yard, the garden of death.[20]

Maturin felt that the fear caused by objects of invisible terror was the most powerful or universal source of emotion;[21] and in the preface to *The Milesian Chief* said he had chosen his own country for the scene because 'I believed it the only country on earth, where from the strange existing opposition of religion, politics and manners, the extremes of refinement and barbarism are united, and the most wild and incredible situations or romantic story are hourly passing before modern eyes.'[22]

And so his Irish novels invested their scenes with these symbolic backgrounds where nature orchestrated the 'incredible situations of romantic story.' After he and Lady Morgan had gothicised the west what could decently follow but a swing to reality in the later nineteenth century? If we read Emily Lawless's *Hurrish*, for instance, we find a careful study of the Burren used to provide us with an isolated community, cliffs convenient for crime, and that almost-to-be-expected sense of the elusive, emotional – even intoxicating – difference distilled by the west of Ireland. Lady Morgan had freely provided us with information enough about the west. One of her heroines for instance, delivered a short lecture to the hero about the question of how the Irish were able to procure so expensive an article as saffron for dying their clothes:

> 'I have heard Father John say', she returned, 'that saffron, as an article of importation, would never have been at any time cheap enough for general use. And I believe formerly, as *now*, they communicated this bright yellow tinge with indigenous plants, with which this country abounds.' 'See', she added, springing lightly forward, and culling a plant which grew from the mountain's side – 'See this little blossom, which they call here, "yellow lady's bed straw", and which you, as a botanist, will better recognise as the *galicens borum*; it communicates a beautiful yellow; as does the *lichen juniperinus*, or "cypress moss" which you brought me yesterday; and I think the *reseda luteola* or "yellow weed" surpasses them all.'[23]

Emily Lawless, however, does the educational job better. She herself gives us omniscient narrator's instruction about the Clare coast, about the Burren, when its beauties were known mainly to the very occasional botanist or local inhabitant. Here, for instance, is her account of these Burren hills which

> are literally not clothed at all. They are startlingly, I may say scandalously, naked. From their base up to the battered turret of rock which serves as a summit, not a patch, not a streak, not an indication even, of green is often to be found in the whole extent. On others a thin sprinkling of grass struggles upward for a few hundred feet, and in valleys and hollows, where the washings of the rocks have accumulated, a grass grows, famous all over cattle-feeding Ireland for its powers of fattening. So, too, in the long vertical rifts or fissures which everywhere cross and recross its surface, maiden-hair ferns and small tender-petalled flowers unfurl, out of reach of the cruel blasts. These do not, however, affect the general impression, which is that of nakedness personified – not comparative, but absolute. The rocks are not scattered over the surface, as in other stony tracts, but the whole surface is rock. They are not hills, in fact, but skeletons – rain-worn, time-worn, wind-worn – starvation made visible, and embodied in a landscape.[24]

23

A. Norman Jeffares

Miss Lawless has no antiquarian delight in the Irish past akin to that of Lady Morgan – she is concerned with the here and now, the passionate events of the Land League and the lawlessness of the eighteen-eighties.[25] And so she writes for an audience which knows quite a little of the history of the country now:

And these strange little hills have had an equally strange history. They were the last home and the last standing-ground of a race whose very names have become a matter of more or less ingenious guess-work. Formorians? Firbolgs? Tuatha da Danaans? Who were they, and what were they? We know nothing, and apparently are not destined to know anything. They came – we know not whence, and they vanished – to all appearance into the Atlantic; pushed westward, like the Norwegian lemming, until, like that most unaccountable of little animals, they, too, sprang into the waves and were lost. Little change has taken place in the aspect of the region since those unknown races passed away. Their great stone-duns are even still in many places the largest buildings to be seen – the oratories and churches which succeeded them having become in their turn, with hardly an exception, ruins like themselves, their very sites forgotten, melted into the surrounding stoniness.[26]

Here the place suits her need to isolate the events, to focus upon how 'the bad days' of the 1880's affected one family, and she writes in a way unlikely to please the present Tourist Board that

The Burren is not – in all probability never will be – a tourist-haunt, but for the few who know it, it has a place apart, a distinct personality – strange, remote, indescribable. Everything that the eye rests on tells us that we are on one of the last standpoints of an old world, worn out with its own profusion, and reduced here to the barest elements. Mother Earth, once young, buxom, frolic-some, is here a wrinkled woman, sitting alone in the evening of her days, and looking with melancholy eyes at the sunset.[27]

There had been a fresh emphasis on place among the nineteenth century poets too. Thomas Moore, for instance, had sent for a copy of Lady Morgan's *Twelve Original Hibernian Melodies* as he was about to issue the first of his own *Irish Melodies*. What he did was

24

to invest Irish place names with plangent sounds, often dwelling on them repetitively: 'Tis Innisfail – 'tis Innisfail' (p. 99).[28] He apostrophised them: 'Sweet Innisfallen fare thee well' (p. 31); 'Silent, Oh Moyle, be the roar of thy water' (p. 47); 'Glendalough, thy gloomy wave/Soon was gentle Kathleen's grave' (p. 39); 'Oh Arranmore, lov'd Arranmore/How oft I dream of thee' (p. 101). He ranged 'from Dinis' green isle to Glena's wooded shore' (p. 39); he celebrated 'the sweet vale of Avoca' (p. 68) as well as 'Tara's halls' (p. 80). And historical events were linked with place:

> Tho' lost to Mononia and cold in the grave
> He returns to Kinkora no more.   (p. 67)

He touched on a perennial problem:

> As vanquish'd Erin wept beside
> The Boyne's illfated river
> She saw where Discord, in the tide,
> Had dropp'd his loaded quiver.   (p. 101)

And, like Lady Morgan, he could, patriotically, link places in the present with even older past Irish history:

> On Lough Neagh's banks as the fisherman strays
> When the clear cold Eve's declining
> He sees the round towers of other days
> In the wave beneath him shining.   (p. 34)

Maria Edgeworth and Lady Morgan both disliked the kind of political climate which followed Daniel O'Connell's era: the day for their kind of writing seemed to them over. The effects of the Young Ireland movement led to a rhetorical poetry, often using round tower, harp, and cromlech as symbols, but generally associating place-names with battles. Literature had become politicised, and, perhaps in reaction against the excesses of this often strident and tired rhetoric, Irish Victorian poets moved to a new kind of local poetry, enjoying the particularity given by naming places, and obviously expecting these names to be evocative in effect. Both William Allingham and Sir Samuel Ferguson wrote of places they loved – combining their description with, in the case of Ferguson's

'Lament for Thomas Davis', a poem filled with new Keatsian combinations of words.[29] Here is the second stanza, on Ballyshannon:

> I sat by Ballyshannon in the summer,
>   And saw the salmon leap,
> And I said as I beheld the gallant creatures
>   Spring glittering from the deep,
> Through the spray and through the prone heaps striving onward
>   To the calm clear streams above,
> So seek'st thou thy native founts of freedom, Thomas Davis,
>   In thy brightness of strength and love!

Allingham used Ballyshannon as the base for an imagined emigrant, and he too includes the salmon in the second stanza of 'The Winding Banks of Erne'.

> No more on pleasant evenings we'll saunter down the Mall,
> When the trout is rising to the fly, the salmon to the fall.
> The boat comes straining on her net, and heavily she creeps,
> Cast off, cast off! – she feels the oars and to her berth she sweeps;
> Now fore and aft keep hauling, and gathering up the clue,
> Till a silver wave of salmon rolls in among the crew. . . .

The third stanza relies on the mentioning of names for its effect:

> The music of the waterfall, the mirror of the tide,
> When all the green-hill'd harbour is full from side to side –
> From Portnasun to Bulliebawns, and round the Abbey Bay,
> From rocky Inis Saimer to Coolnargit sandhills grey;
> While far upon the southern line, to guard it like a wall,
> The Leitrim mountains, clothed in blue, gaze calmly over all.

Yeats, profoundly influenced by both writers, originally thought of writing poems about Sligo as Allingham had about Ballyshannon. He saw Sligo shut in, cut off from the world, a secret area enclosed and protected by the Curlew Hills – an impression reinforced no doubt by his own journeyings there by sea in his grandfather's ships. His early poetry reminds us of Emily Lawless's Mother Earth – a Western 'wrinkled woman looking with melancholy eyes at the sunset.' Why should the sunset be thus associated with melan-

26

cholia? Is the image of the sun setting over water *per se* more intense in effect, more likely to stir thoughts of mortality and the limitations of earthly life? Yeats certainly used this imagery often in his early melancholic twilight poetry, being conscious, in Sligo, of how 'the sun drops down in the tide.'[30] Another phrase, 'The red sun falls and the world grows dim'[31] may seem neutral enough were we not guided to respond to the melancholic suggestions made in this context by his adjective 'dim'; the language of *The Wanderings of Oisin* stresses the decay of the sun: 'In the pale west and the sun's rim sank'[32] (or 'now in the sea the sun's rim sank').[33] And in 'Cuchulain's Fight with the Sea', he remarked that 'the sun falls into the western deep.'[34] Sligo, of these dramatic sunsets, these sinkings of the sun into the western sea, was a magical place, a place of mystery, not least because many of Yeats's middle-aged memories centred upon its beauty, as in old age it held his fiercer attention.

Emily Lawless, too, had been able to imbue scenery with sinister aspects earlier on, as when she described an all too brief happy moment, in *Hurrish* but added:

> The evening was closing in, the sun sinking like a red-hot cannon-ball into the grey, cool breast of the Atlantic. . . .[35]

There was indeed something sinister about it, as even old Bridget realised:

> The western sky was clear, and almost colourless, but upon the other side, beyond the interesting Burren hills, it was a mass of finely graduated colour. A multitude of arrowy flames, like the *dijecta* of some aerial volcano, were shooting their fiery points, one after the other, in a continuous flight across the zenith. . . .[36]

'Red as the devil! red as the devil! ' was Bridget's response to this sunset, and Alley, the innocent girl heroine-victim of the story suddenly experienced a sense of impending trouble. Agrarian violence was about to erupt again, and with it the violence which would overwhelm Hurrish and all his family.

To a certain extent, Emily Lawless was bound to utilise the scenery of the Burren: it was as though she had set violence moving in the area and it took on its own wild life within this stark setting.

27

Similarly Yeats had set melancholic wistful beauty into his early Sligo poetry – naming the names of places in poems, and then in 'The Lake Isle' succumbing to the general escapist as well as particular nostalgic appeal of the place itself (like Goldsmith, earlier, also writing about Ireland in London). He moved from local to national poetry, the legends peopling the places, and then as he became his own legend he rooted himself into the western scene in County Galway and into the continuous backward looking processes of Irish history as he inherited his tower's memories of its earlier owners.

To him the west offered a way back into the saner life of an oral tradition. No matter that he did not understand the Gaelic of Galway; he knew that there was still

upon these great level plains a people, a community bound together by imaginative possessions, by stories and poems which have grown out of its own life, and by a past of great passions which can still waken the heart to imaginative action.[37]

These ideas were prompted by a day when he stood on the side of Slieve Echtge looking out over Galway:

The Burren Hills were to my left, and though I forget whether I could see the cairn over Bald Conan of the Fianna, I could certainly see many places there that are in poems and stories. In front of me, over many miles of level Galway plains, I saw a low blue hill flooded with evening light. I asked a countryman who was with me what hill that was, and he told me it was Cruachmaa of the Sidhe. I had often heard of Cruachmaa of the Sidhe even as far north as Sligo, for the country people have told me a great many stories of the great host of the Sidhe who live there, still fighting and holding festivals.[38]

Yeats peopled the west with mythological figures. For Joyce, perhaps, it contained more recent, historical people: those whom Cromwell had pushed there, those romantic, passionate people whence his wife Nora Barnacle came. Something of this is contained in the one word 'mutinous' which so reverberates for Irish readers back, into and through that reverberating story 'The Dead'. Michael Furey, from Oughterard, who had loved Gretta, who had died of a decline, who had died of love for her, who had sung 'The Lass of Augrim' for her – significantly linking person and place – seemed to Gabriel, Gretta's husband, mysterious, someone who had passed into that other world in the full glory of passion. Joyce moves near Yeats here: 'For a moment Gabriel's soul had approached that region where dwell the vast hosts of the dead.' And then the snow falls all over Ireland and we realise how significant it is that Gabriel is an easterner (a Dubliner, surely, since his father worked for the Port and Docks Board and he himself was a graduate of the Royal University in Dublin) to whom the west remains mysterious, even unpleasant. At the party he had remarked that he preferred to spend his holidays on the continent; he did not want to go west to learn Gaelic there; Irish was not his language, he said; and he replied shortly to a query about his wife being from Connaught with: 'Her people are'. But the snow was general all over Ireland; it

was falling on every part of the dark central plain, on the treeless hills, falling softly upon the Bog of Allen and farther westward, softly falling into the dark mutinous Shannon waves.[39]

Crossing the Shannon, the natural boundary for the west, was a move westwards which, for the Anglo-Irish writer, often signified romance and adventure. Synge, for instance, found himself – found his strength as a writer – in the world of the Aran Islands, and Lady Gregory, not then knowing him, disliked the very sight of him, his presence there, seeing him as an interloper in that archaic world she too was seeking to enter and to understand. On the other hand George Moore felt he understood the west only too well;[40] but then he had grown up wanting to get away from Moore Hall. The western world was understood by Douglas Hyde in a different, more comfortable way – perhaps because, unlike Moore, he had taught himself Irish. To read his early diaries is to realise that some reactions to place have an essentially practical side. He describes bog land precisely, economically, just as Lord Dunsany produced one of the best descriptions of a red bog ever penned, both of them reacting to the home of snipe or woodcock with a sportsman's eye.

And here we must acknowledge the use of scenery made by novelists or poets who take it for granted, who describe it, who create it, as the needs of their material dictate. Somerville and Ross, for instance, show the range this permits. In *Sarah's Youth* we get a Hyde-Dunsany passage from a hunting point of view:

> Out of the brilliant sunshine of the lawn in front of the Castle, the little cavalcade passed into the gloom of the back avenue, a narrow road shrouded by yews and laurels, that led to a wild and wide space of hill and moorland known as the Craugh Mor, a wilderness of many acres in extent, dedicated to foxes, and badgers, rabbits, and young cattle, and little black-faced mountain sheep, chosen winter quarters for woodcock and snipe; with a big plantation of fir trees covering a long flank of the nearer hill, and everywhere great tracts of furze and rock and bog. Above the fir-wood lay a small and secret lake, fed by a fierce stream that rose among farther hills, and came racing down from the heights to degenerate at length, in the low-lying lands, into the sluggish *Caol* which Sarah and Tim Kavanagh had jumped on the memorable day when Judy the grey mare changed hands. It was a chosen meet for holiday lookers-on, but a hard one on hounds and horses.[41]

Yet again, however, when Sarah begins to grow up at the end of the novel the scenery, of the mid-April day, chimes with her mood:

> . . . the furze, in full bloom, was blazing with the splendour that is a yearly miracle. All the crooked, wandering fences that divide Southern Irish fields, as in no other civilised country fields are divided, were crested with burning gold, spring's largesse that she unfailingly flings to a poor country. The fox-covert that faced the Shruell avenue gates was a sheet of what looked like consolidated sunlight. The scent, which is like the scent of apricots, was all-pervading. The lucent sky of fickle April had a long wing of wood-pigeon grey cloud, edged with silver, lying across it in the west, just a gentle threat of a possible shower. It merged into a bank of what looked like tumbled snow, against which the hills of the horizon leaned, lavender-blue. It was a day to rise the heart, and Sarah, without knowing it, felt its magic.[42]

Different is the setting, for a darker story, in *An Irish Cousin*. The general tone of the book is set almost casually in Maturin's vein:

I went upstairs with the feeling of isolation again strongly upon me. The wind had risen, and on the walls of the draughty corridor each gust made the old pictures shake in their shabby frames. At intervals, through the panes of the large skylight overhead, the moon's light dropped in pale wavering squares on the floor of the hall below. I leaned over the balustrades, watching the spectral alternations of light and darkness, as the clouds swept across the moon, till the objects beneath me seemed to take intermitting motion from the flitting of the moonbeams.

As I looked, the dim lamp in the hall flickered and went out. A gust from below circled round the corridor, lifting the hair upon my forehead and almost extinguishing my candle as it passed me.

Perhaps I was overtired and nervous, but the old childish dread of some vague pursuit out of the darkness clutched me. I gave a terrified glance over my shoulder at the swaying pictures, then, shielding my candle with my hand, I ignominiously ran down the corridor into my own room.[43]

The ironic moment of the novel comes as the grey continuous flood of rain begins to cease and the wind shifts:

By luncheon-time the rain had nearly spent itself. The wind went round into the north-west, and a wet gleam of sunshine suddenly shone out on the trees, making every branch and twig show with pale distinctness against the bank of purple cloud behind. A pilot-boat was beating in to Durrusmore Harbour in the teeth of the cold wind; the curlews screamed fitfully as they flew inland. It was not a pleasant afternoon, but I was thankful for the chance of getting out of the house.

The shubberies were chilly and dripping, and their walks were covered with soaking withered leaves, but they were sheltered from the wind. I had come to the place where I had once left the path to gather ferns by the stream, when, at the angle where the two paths meet, I came suddenly upon Willy.[44]

Willy has ruined his life and his father vanishes into the wood:

Last year's briars grew thick and strong in the woods, fencing the drenched thickets of dead bracken. The paths were slippery

31

with mud, the deep stillness was full of secrecy and hopelessness. Fallen trees, victims of the storm of two days ago, barred my aimless rangings with their prone branches, and the muddy pits from which their roots had been torn had, in many places, swallowed up the paths. I do not know how long or how far I wandered in the delusive network of tracks, but I was aware that wherever I climbed, or struggled, or waded, Roche was not far from me. Every now and then he called to me; it was obvious that he did not mean to leave me alone. The messengers that he had sent forth for help had brought back reinforcements; from the number of voices calling to each other it seemed that there must be by this time about twenty or thirty men engaged in the search. They were in the big woods on the farther side of the house, advancing in line, like beaters.[45]

Perhaps, however, the best moments in Irish life, literary and actual, are – because of the generally vagarious nature of the climate – those of picnics. Short or long, they encapsulate the beauty of the place, they indicate the brevity of life, and the long careful art of some writers has captured their ethos. Somerville and Ross, again, in the picnic by a quarry, or yet again in those humanly painful but naturally beautiful days in *The Real Charlotte*, delight in scenery. Take a characteristic passage such as this:

The lake was narrower here, where it neared the end of its twenty-mile span, and so calm that the sheep and cattle grazing on the brown mountains were reflected in its depths, and the yacht seemed as incongruous in the midst of them as the ark on Mount Ararat. The last bend of the lake was before them; the *Daphne* crept round it, moved mysteriously by wind that was imperceptible to the baking company on the steam-launch, and by the time the latter had churned her way round the fir-clad point, the yacht was letting go her anchor near the landing-place of a large wooded island.

At a picnic nothing is of much account before luncheon, and the gloom of hunger hung like a pall over the party that took ashore luncheon baskets, unpacked knives and forks, and gathered stones to put on the corners of the table-cloth. But such a hunger is Nature's salve for the inadequacy of human beings to amuse themselves; the body comes to the relief of the mind with the compassionate superiority of a good servant, and confers inward festivity upon many a dull dinner party.[46]

They extract humour from the contrast between natural beauty and human behaviour; they realise that

. . . there is something unavoidably vulgar in the aspect of a picnic party when engaged in the culminating rite of eating on the grass. They may feel themselves to be picturesque, gipsy-like, even romantic, but to the unparticipating looker-on, not even the gilded dignity of champagne can redeem them from being a mere group of greedy, huddled backs, with ugly trimmings of paper, dirty plates, and empty bottles. But at Innishochery the only passers-by were straight-flying wild-duck or wood pigeons, or an occasional sea-gull lounging up from the distant Atlantic, all observant enough in their way, but not critical. It is probable they did not notice even the singular ungracefulness of Miss Mullen's attitude, as she sat with her short legs uncomfortably tucked away, and her large jaws moving steadily as she indemnified herself for the stupidity of the recent trip.[47]

Besides picnics, there are excursions. Hawkins, the flirtatious subaltern, smitten by Francie, takes her on an expedition in the steam launch. Space is emphasised particularly, as in the earlier passage quoted, by reflections in the water, and this expanded space creates an expansion in time; in this case, the extension of time given by the space is disastrous.

The posting of a letter, which he had fortunately found in his pocket, had been the pretext for the expedition, and both he and Francie confidently believed that they would get back to Bruff at about six o'clock. It is true that Mr Hawkins received rather a shock when, on arriving at Lismoyle, he found that it was already six o'clock, but he kept this to himself, and lost no time in starting again for Bruff.

The excitement and hurry of the escapade had conspired, with the practical business of steering and attending to the various brass taps, to throw sentiment for a space into the background, and that question as to whether forgiveness should or should not

33

be extended to him, hung enchantingly on the horizon, as delightful and as seductive as the blue islands that floated far away in the yellow haze of the lowered sun. There was not a breath of wind, and the launch slit her way through tranquil, oily spaces of sky that lay reflected, deep in the water, and shaved the long rocky points so close that they could see the stones at the bottom looking like enormous cairngorms in the golden shallows.

'That was a near thing', remarked Mr Hawkins complacently, as a slight grating sound told that they had grazed one of these smooth-backed monsters.[48]

Of course, they do run aground and scandal is caused. Francie marries Lambert, but Hawkins reappears, due to leave on his posting in ten days. And space can provide room for foolishness; it is something into which humans can expand too rashly:

At the back of the Rosemount kitchen-garden the ground rose steeply into a knoll of respectable height, where grew a tangle of lilac bushes, rhododendrons, syringas, and yellow broom. A gravel path wound ingratiatingly up through these, in curves artfully devised by Mr Lambert to make the most of the extent and the least of the hill, and near the top a garden-seat was sunk in the bank, with laurels shutting it in on each side, and a laburnum 'showering golden tears' above it. Through the perfumed screen of the lilac bushes in front unromantic glimpses of the roof of the house were obtainable – eyesores to Mr Lambert, who had concentrated all his energies on hiding everything nearer than the semi-circle of lake and distant mountain held in an opening cut through the rhododendrons at the corner of the little plateau on which the seat stood. Without the disturbance of middle distance the eye lay at ease on the far-off struggle of the Connemara mountains, and on a serene vista of Lough Moyle; a view that enticed forth, as to a playground, the wildest and most foolish imaginations, and gave them elbow-room; a world so large and remote that it needed the sound of wheels on the road to recall the existence of the petty humanities of Lismoyle.

Francie and Hawkins were sitting there on the afternoon of the day on which Lambert was expected to come home, and as the sun, that had stared in at them through the opening in the rhododendrons when they first went there, slid farther round,

34

their voices sank in unconscious accord with the fading splendours of the afternoon, and their silences seemed momently more difficult to break.[49]

Again, the description in Chapter XLVII of the old turf quay at Bruff may seem at first to be a *jeu d'esprit*, a self-indulgent purple patch. Here it is:

The stems of the lilies that curved up through its brown-golden depths were visible almost down to the black mud out of which their mystery of silver and gold was born; and, while the water outside moved piquantly to the breeze, nothing stirred it within except the water spiders, who were darting about, pushing a little ripple in front of them, and finding themselves seriously inconvenienced by the pieces of broken rush and the sodden fragments of turf that perpetually stopped their way. It had rained and blown very hard all the day before, and the innermost corners of the tiny harbour held a motionless curve of foam, yellowish brown, and flecked with the feathers of a desolated moorhen's nest.

Civilisation at Bruff had marched away from the turf quay. The ruts of the cart-track were green from long disuse and the willows had been allowed to grow across it, as a last sign of superannuation. In old days every fire at Bruff had been landed at the turf quay from the bogs at the other side of the lake; but now, since the railway had come to Lismoyle, coal had taken its place. It was in vain that Thady the turf-cutter had urged that turf was a far handsomer thing about a gentleman's place than coal. The last voyage of the turf boat had been made, and she now lay, grey from rottenness and want of paint, in the corner of the miniature dock that had once been roofed over and formed a boat-house. Tall, jointed reeds, with their spiky leaves and stiff stems, stood out in the shallow water, leaning aslant over their own reflections, and, further outside, green rushes grew quickly in long beds, the homes of dab-chicks, coots, and such like water people. Standing on the brown rock that formed the end of the quay, the spacious sky was so utterly reproduced in the lake, cloud for cloud, deep for deep, that it only required a little imagination to believe oneself floating high between two atmospheres.[50]

35

Here is Anglo-Irish space *par excellence:* it should create peace, but again and again Somerville and Ross remind us that there is dissonance; for life, quite simply, includes it.

> The young herons, in the fir trees on Curragh Point, were giving utterance to their meditations on things in general in raucous monosyllables, and Charlotte Mullen, her feet planted firmly on two of the least rickety stones of the quay, was continuing a conversation that had gone on one-sidedly for some time.[51]

Charlotte Mullen is wrecking Roddy Lambert's life; she is denouncing him to Christopher Dysart, and we are shown her nature in part by the contrast between her and this exquisite place. After her speech, the narrators gently show us why they had evoked this atmosphere of unspoiled, idyllic, time-stopped beauty.

> 'Yes, Sir Christopher, my feeling for your estate is like the feeling of a child for the place where he was reared; it is the affection of a woman whose happiest days were passed with her father in your estate office! '
> The accurate balance of the sentence and its nasal cadence showed that Charlotte was delivering herself of a well-studied peroration. Her voice clashed with the stillness as dissonantly as the clamour of the young herons. Her face was warm and shiny, and Christopher looked away from it, and said to himself that she was intolerable.[52]

Perhaps the most lyrical and evocative use of natural beauty in Anglo-Irish literature is to be found in George Moore's *The Lake*. Here space means isolation, and here in the opening moments of the novel the priest is powerfully affected by the beauty of the May morning. The lake is like a mirror: 'The ducks were talking softly in the reeds, the reeds themselves were talking and the water lapped softly above the smooth limestone shores.' Every man has a lake in his heart, says the priest, feeling like an instrument that had been tuned. Later in the novel his perception

> . . . seemed to have been indefinitely increased, and it seemed to him as if he were in communion with the stones in the earth and

36

the clouds in heaven; it seemed to him as if the past and the future had become one.

The moment was one of extraordinary sweetness; never might such a moment happen in his life again. The earth and sky were enfolding in one tender harmony of rose and blue, the blue shading down to grey, and the lake floated amid vague shores, vaguely as a dream floats through sleep. The swallows were flying high, quivering overhead in the blue air. There was a sense of security and persuasion and loveliness in the evening.[53]

This is what the Irish writer realises Irish space can do for him or his characters; it can take them out of time, out of the past – a thing particularly to be hoped for – into a blessed sense of time-lessness, the Traherne-like vision, the present that perhaps only children really know. And even they need space for it, for if one has space enough, then one has time enough. Joyce Cary, my final author, in *A House of Children*, has captured superbly that sense of having time enough which is true timelessness – something that those whose childhood holidays resembled his in Donegal will always value, something (let us hope) that Ireland will keep un-spoiled for future children: the wonder of empty, blessedly un-developed space.

There is no more beautiful view in the world than that great lough, seventy square miles of salt water, from the mountains of Annish. We had heard my father call it beautiful, and so we enjoyed it with our minds as well as our feelings; keenly with both together. Wherever we went in Annish we were among the mountains and saw the lough or the ocean; often, from some high place, the whole Annish peninsula, between the two great loughs; and the Atlantic, high up in the sky, seeming like a moun-tain of water higher than the tallest of land. So that my memories are full of enormous skies, as bright as water, in which clouds sailed bigger than any others; fleets of monsters moving in one vast school up from the horizon and over my head, a million miles up, as it seemed to me, and then down again over the far-off mountains of Derry. They seemed to follow a curving surface of air concentric with the curve of the Atlantic which I could see bending down on either hand, a bow, which, even as a child of three or four, I knew to be the actual shape of the earth. Some grown-up, perhaps my father, had printed that upon my imagination, so that even while I was playing some childish game in the heather, red Indians or Eskimos, if I caught sight of the ocean with the tail of my eye, I would feel suddenly the roundness and independence of the world beneath me. I would feel it like a ship under my feet moving through air just like a larger stiffer cloud, and this gave me an extraordinary exhilaration.[54]

We travelled through this enormous and magnificent scene in tranquil happiness. We were tired from running about in the heather and already growing hungry we felt the nearness of supper, and bed, with the calm faith which belongs only to children and saints devoted to the love of God and sure of the delights of communing with him. In that faith, that certainty of coming joys, we existed in a contentment so profound that it was like a lazy kind of drunkenness. I can't count how many times I enjoyed that sense, riding in a sidecar whose swaying motion would have put me to sleep if I had not been obliged to hold on; so that while my body and head and legs were all swinging together in a half dream, my hand tightly clutched some other child's body; and the memory of bathing, shouting, tea, the blue smoke of picnic fires, was mixed with the dark evening clouds shaped like flying geese, the tall water stretching up to the top of the world, the mountains sinking into darkness like whales into the ocean and over all a sky so deep that the stars, faint green sparks, seemed lost in it and the very sense of it made the heart light and proud, like a bird.[55]

NOTES

1 Jonathan Swift, *Poetical Works,* ed. Herbert Davis (London, 1967), p. 331.
2 *Ibid.,* p. 390.
3 *Ibid.,* p. 465.
4 Jonathan Swift, *Journal to Stella,* ed. Harold Williams (Oxford, 1948), I, 220.
5 *The Poems of Gray, Collins and Goldsmith,* ed. Roger Lonsdale (London, 1969), p. 676.
6 *Memoirs of Richard Lovell Edgeworth Esq.* (London, 1820), II, 5.
7 *Ibid.,* II, 8.

8   *Ibid.*, II, 11.

9   *Ibid.*, II, 317.

10 *Ibid.*, II, 232.

11 Lady Morgan (Sydney Owenson), *The Life of Salvator Rosa* (London, 1824), p. iii.

12 Sydney Owenson, *The Wild Irish Girl* (London, 1805); text from Colburn's Standard Edition, 'edited by Lady Morgan', 1846, p. 26.

13 *Ibid.*, p. 25.

14 *Ibid.*, p. 56. In this edition, the 'groves' are replaced by 'a wood', and the 'lakes' by 'a lake': the 1805 London and the 1807 Philadelphia editions were more exuberant products of Sydney Owenson's enthusiasm, which Lady Morgan sobered up in her editing of her early work for the 1846 edition.

15 Charles Maturin, *The Milesian Chief* (London, 1812), II, 185.

16 *Ibid.*, I, 55.

17 *Irish Quarterly Review*, March 1852, II, 146.

18 Charles Maturin, *Women, or Pour et Contre* (Edinburgh and London, 1818), II, 62-3.

19 *Ibid.*, II, 38.

20 Charles Maturin, *Melmoth the Wanderer* (Edinburgh and London, 1820), I, 51-2.

21 Charles Maturin, Preface to *Montorio*, p. v.

22 Charles Maturin, Preface to *The Milesian Chief*, p. v.

23 Sydney Owenson, *The Wild Irish Girl* (1846), p. 153.

24 Emily Lawless, *Hurrish, A Study* (London, 1895), p. 2.

25 A subject also well treated by George Moore in *A Drama in Muslin* where the countryside in 'a disturbed state' is a sombre backdrop to the tinsel of the Viceregal court in Dublin.

26 Emily Lawless, *Hurrish*, p. 2.

27 *Ibid.*, p. 3.

28 References for this and subsequent melodies are given from *Moore's Irish Melodies* . . . with a memoir by J. F. Waller, n.d.

29 The texts of poems by Ferguson and Allingham have been taken from *Irish Poets of the Nineteenth Century*, ed. Geoffrey Taylor (Muses' Library, 1951), pp. 140-44 and 32-7.

30 W. B. Yeats, *Poems* (1895), *The Wanderings of Oisin*, I, line 9.

31 W. B. Yeats, *Poems* (2 volume edition, 1949), *The Wanderings of Oisin*, I, line 105.

32 *Ibid.*, I, line 153.

33 *The Wanderings of Oisin* (1889), line 153.

34 *Poems* (1895), line 34.

35 *Hurrish*, p. 269.

36 *Ibid.*, p. 269.

37 W. B. Yeats, 'The Galway Plains', *Essays and Introductions* (London, 1961), p. 213.

38 *Ibid.*, p. 211.

39 James Joyce, *Dubliners* (London, Penguin edition, 1956), p. 220.

40 His comments on the west in *Parnell and his Island* are worth reading in this connection.

41 Somerville and Ross, *Sarah's Youth* (1938), p. 182.
42 *Ibid.*, p. 307.
43 Somerville and Ross, *An Irish Cousin* (revised edition, 1903), pp. 29-30.
44 *Ibid.*, p. 272.
45 *Ibid.*, p. 299.
46 Somerville and Ross, *The Real Charlotte* (World's Classics, 1948), pp. 113-4.
47 *Ibid.*, p. 114.
48 *Ibid.*, pp. 228-9.
49 *Ibid.*, pp. 482-3.
50 *Ibid.*, p. 470.
51 *Ibid.*, pp. 470-1.
52 *Ibid.*, p. 471.
53 George Moore, *The Lake* (London, 1905), p. 267.
54 Joyce Cary, *A House of Children* (Carfax edition, 1951), pp. 18-19.
55 *Ibid.*, p. 20.

RETURN TO THE HEARTHSTONE: IDEALS OF THE CELTIC LITERARY REVIVAL

ROBERT O'DRISCOLL

> In a little time places may begin to seem the only hieroglyphs that cannot be forgotten, and poets to remember that they will come the nearer the old poets, who had a seat at every hearth, if they mingle their own dream with a story told for centuries. . . . – W. B. YEATS.

I

Before the flowering of the Celtic Literary Revival at the end of the nineteenth century, there had been much conscious and unconscious preparation for the movement. In those crevices of significant soil that progress and industrialization had passed by and where the Irish language was still spoken, Celtic traditions survived, traditions in music, myth, ar d folklore that stretched back hundreds, and some of them even thousands of years to pre-Christian and pre-Roman times: successive invasions by the Vikings, Normans, and English had in many ways left the native culture undisturbed. But in the parts of Ireland that had not chosen the weapons of silence and exile for self-preservation, those parts of the country that, through force, necessity or expediency, had adopted the tongue of their temporary conquerors, the great Celtic traditions that had been the heritage of their ancestors were, to all intents and purposes, lost. There were, of course, points of contact, but as time progressed the Celtic civilization slipped further and further out of the literary and historical consciousness of the modern world, until in the nineteenth century the civilization was dramatically re-discovered: to many it was not a discovery but a revelation.

James Macpherson was in some ways the catalyst for this rediscovery, producing during the 1760's his Ossianic translations

41

which, as every undergraduate knows, were forgeries, though they purported to be authentic translations of a third-century poet. Nevertheless, Macpherson's work did open up Celtic literature to English and European attention, and caught off guard some scholars and historians who went so far as to deny the existence of any Celtic civilization whatsoever: the Scottish historian, John Pinkerton, for example, writes in 1789:

> The former [the Irish antiquaries] say, their country was highly civilized, had letters and academies, as the Greeks and Romans. The latter [the European antiquaries] say, the Greeks we know, and the Romans we know, but who are ye? Those Greeks and Romans pronounce you not only barbarous, but utterly savage. Where are your authorities against this? In the name of that degree of rationality, which even some beasts have, where are the slightest marks of civilization among you? Where are ruins of cities? Where inscriptions? Where ancient art or science in your whole island? The old inhabitants of your country, the Wild Irish, the true Milesian breed, untainted with Gothic blood, we know to be utter savages at this day. Can a nation, once civilized, ever become savage? Impossible! [1]

The nineteenth century witnessed the gradual recovery of the Celtic civilization: it was a century of painstaking research and of imaginative flashes. Early Christian artefacts and treasures of the Bronze Age were discovered; coins and inscriptions were studied and historical records published; pioneering topographical, archaeological, and architectural investigations were conducted; philologists began to study the Irish language in its broader Indo-European context; the ancient Brehon laws were published and traditional Irish music rescued; poems in the Irish language were translated, and their metrical patterns and idioms introduced for the first time in English; Celtic legends were edited and the first expository poems based on Celtic myth were written. There were, as I say, a few flashes: by the Unionist Ferguson, who began his investigation of the literary legacy of his Catholic countrymen as an intellectual curiosity and was led into an imaginative immersion in the past: by Mangan who, in his achievement of self-expression by a passionate identification with past heroes and crucial moments in his country's history, knew instinctively the mythic mode; and by Standish James

O'Grady, whose *History of Ireland* presented an imaginative reconstruction of early Celtic life and made the heroic period and
mythic characters 'once again a portion of the imagination of the
country.'[2] O'Grady's *History*, Yeats writes, did more 'than anything else to create that preoccupation with Irish folk-lore and
legend and epic which is called the Irish literary movement.'[3]

II

From the faltering, painstaking, and sometimes intuitive work of
the nineteenth-century poets, antiquaries, and historians to the
full critical and artistic articulation of the ideals of the Celtic
Revival was a great imaginative leap. This leap of the imagination
was accomplished by the two poets and visionaries who were the
spiritual leaders of the Revival, W. B. Yeats and George Russell
(AE), and in exploring the ideals of the Revival I shall illustrate
my arguments now from the one writer, now from the other:
indeed, so close are their ideas that it is sometimes difficult to
indicate where the first articulation of a particular perception
originates.

It is difficult to say at what precise point, and in what circumstances, the being or genius or deity that shapes a national character enters once again the poetic and popular consciousness.[4] What
one can say is that almost from the beginning of their creative
careers Yeats and AE recognized what they had been chosen to
accomplish: they believed themselves to be mediums chosen to
express the uncreated consciousness of their race, and the movement they created was not 'a self-conscious endeavour to make a
literature,' but the spontaneous expression of an impulse that had
been gathering power for centuries.[5] In the beginning of all important things, Yeats writes, 'there is a moment when we understand more perfectly than we understand again until all is finished.'[6]
Yeats and AE cannot be dismissed as being involved in a kind of
provincial primitivism, or of concerning themselves with Celtic
lore and legend in order to give their work local colour: what they
deliberately set out to accomplish was to lay the spiritual and intellectual foundation of the modern Irish nation, to make what was
instinctive, and on the point of being lost, part of conscious art,
and, by extension, once again a living part of the national consciousness.

III

For Yeats and AE, frontiers, boundaries, race, language, religion, or even blood do not define or constitute a nation: the bonds that bind a people into a nation are not physical but 'psychic'. A nation, AE writes, is 'a collective imagination held with intensity, an identity of culture or consciousness among millions, which makes them act as a single entity in relation to other human groups.'[7] Neither is a nation the creation of practical parliamentarians or politicians: centuries of subjective life and brooding thought precede its creation, and the true architects of a nation are artists, the heroes of history, and the figures of mythology:

> A nation exists primarily because of its own imagination of itself. It is a spirit created by the poets, historians, musicians, by the utterances of great men, the artists in life. The mysterious element of beauty, of a peculiar beauty, exists in every nation and is the root cause of the love felt for it by the citizens, just as the existence of spirit, the most mysterious and impalpable thing, is the fountain of the manifold activities of the body.[8]

The figures of mythology, these writers suggest, are not an individual creation, but the communal creation of the people themselves, 'through a slow process of modification and adaptation,' to express their ideals and their passions, their loves and their hates.[9] For AE the figures of mythology are a gift from heaven: they 'come out of the spirit,' descending 'from the heaven-world of the imagination into the national being.'[10] It makes little difference whether these figures had any historical existence, whether they ever lived in a physical sense: the fact is that they have lived in the national consciousness, and to generation after generation, brooding and recounting their fantastic deeds, they are living presences, 'as real', AE claims, 'as flesh and blood.'[11]

The heroes of history also contribute to the national being: when they die, their heroic acts pass from earth and become part of the 'immortal memory' of the nation, chiefly because of the dramatic or artistic quality of the acts themselves, or because of the way in which the heroes and their heroic acts are mythologized by the artist. Art is, therefore, the agency through which the essence of a nation 'filters into [the] national consciousness,'[12] and the artist is an instrument by which the heroes of history and the figures of mythology become living presences in the mind of the people: nothing is more important in the life of a nation 'than the images which haunt the minds of its people, for it is by these they are led to act.'[13] Imagination, AE writes, whether 'spiritual or national, is the most powerful thing in human affairs. Intangible itself, it moves bodies. Invisible itself, it changes visible civilizations.'[14] The artist too, when his work is done, enters the national imagination, is consumed into the dance or trance of his own art: 'the poetry of Yeats,' AE writes, 'is the greatest spiritual gift any Irishman has made to his tribe.'[15] And elsewhere AE suggests that Yeats and the writers of the Celtic Revival 'will act through many men and women, and the birth of their imaginations will be as important in the evolution of Irish character and nationality as the fight in Easter week.'[16]

A nation, therefore, is a living entity constituted 'of immortal deeds and heroic spirits, influencing the living, a life within their life, moulding their spirits to its likeness.'[17] Every heroic deed in the life of a nation is an act of the spirit; every perception of beauty by an artist or visionary brings the divine essence animating the nation closer to the articulated consciousness of the people, until by a sequence of heroic acts and artistic perceptions the 'accumulated beauty' of the ages becomes more compelling than the necessities of daily life: 'the dream . . . [begins] to enter into the children of our race, and their thoughts turn from earth to that [divine] world in which it had its inception.'[18]

IV

For the writers of the Celtic Revival the roots of Irish Nationality ran deep, deeper than the events that have shaped the Western world: the Roman Empire, Christianity, and the Renaissance. 'Behind all Irish history,' Yeats writes, 'hangs a great tapestry, even Christianity had to accept it and be itself pictured there. Nobody looking at its dim folds can say where Christianity begins and Druidism ends.'[19] And in his lecture with the arresting title, 'The Necessity of De-Anglicizing Ireland,' Douglas Hyde writes, rather flamboyantly, that behind the expression of Irish nationality

is the half unconscious feeling that the race which at one time held possession of more than half Europe, which established itself in Greece, and burned infant Rome, is now – almost extirpated and absorbed elsewhere – making its last stand for independence in this island of Ireland; and do what they may the race of today cannot wholly divest itself from the mantle of its own past. Through early Irish literature, for instance, can we best form some conception of what that race really was, which, after overthrowing and trampling on the primitive peoples of half Europe, was itself forced in turn to yield its speech, manners, and independence to the victorious eagles of Rome. We alone of the nations of Western Europe escaped the claws of those birds of prey; we alone developed ourselves naturally upon our own lines outside of and free from all Roman influence; we alone were thus able to produce an early art and literature, *our* antiquities can best throw light upon the pre-Romanised inhabitants of half Europe. . . . The dim consciousness of this is one of those things which are at the back of Irish national sentiment, and our business, whether we be Unionists or Nationalists, should be to make this dim consciousness an active and potent feeling. . . .[20]

The Celtic civilization, Yeats and Hyde and AE contended, was unique in Europe because it had escaped the yoke of the Roman Empire, the secularization of the Renaissance, and, perhaps more importantly, the material domination of the Anglo-Saxon world. But Ireland, although achieving an advanced civilization when the rest of Europe was plunged in darkness, had, at the end of the nineteenth century, not yet been born as a modern state, as a collective political unit, the reason for this being the cultural, political, and economic oppression the Irish had suffered at the hands of the British. Throughout these centuries of oppression, however, Ireland had never lost the consciousness of herself as an independent entity, and of her essential difference from the English nation.

V

The difference between the two nations was clearly apprehended by the leaders of the Celtic Revival. The English nation, they argued, had been shaped on the principles of imperial domination and material success,[21] and although the incorporated ideals of the Italian Renaissance had brought to England a sense of personality and a new emphasis on the capabilities of man, they had, when subsumed into the Anglo-Saxon mentality, resulted in a scientific approach to the world, imperialism, materialism, industrialization, urbanization, and collectivization.[22]

Imperialism, whether it be of the visible physical kind practised by England from the seventeenth to the twentieth century, or of the subtle, even more effective, invisible variety being successfully pursued by several world powers today, imposes on the individual or nation the model of another people, and insists that all citizens have 'their minds poured into the same mould,' and that 'varieties of gifts' and distinctive cultural traditions be obliterated.[23] This imposition of an imperialist ideal was rejected by the writers of the Celtic Revival long before the political and military leaders created a physical body for the spiritual principles:

> Empires do not permit the intensive cultivation of human life: . . . they destroy the richness and variety of existence by the extinction of peculiar and unique gifts, and the substitution therefore of a culture which has its value mainly for the people who created it, but is as alien to our race as the mood of the scientist is to the artist or poet.[24]

Imperialism and materialism are closely linked. Materialism is built on the belief that matter is the sole reality, that only the limited life of the body is real, that there is no essential difference between the natural and spiritual order, and that knowledge can be discovered through observation of the external world and the analysis of impressions derived from the five senses. Materialism contracts man's consciousness by limiting him to personal experience. Because it originates in egotism, in action for the consequences of action, and for the acquisition of possessions, materialism must conclude in rigid laws, barbed-wire fences, and conspiracies.

The principles of imperialism and materialism had, Yeats and AE contended, affected the development of English literature. In the first place, English literature had no native mythology. Shakespeare had, of course, used English history as the subject of some of his plays, and had there been no Renaissance and no Italian

47

influence, English history might, Yeats contends, 'have become as important to the English imagination as the Greek myths to the Greek imagination.'[25] When they attempted to use myth to express their own personalities, English writers looked therefore to Greece, Rome, or the land of the Bible, to myths of foreign lands, and to myths that had grown threadbare with use, until by the time a William Blake emerged, he was, in Yeats's words, 'a man crying out for a mythology,' and having no national myths, he had to invent his own.[26] England, of course, had over the centuries produced a great literature, but it was a literature of the few that had been shaped almost completely by the printing-press, and during the nineteenth century England succumbed to what Yeats called the 'cold, joyless, irreligious' scientific movement.[27] Nineteenth-century English novels and the poetry of Wordsworth, Tennyson, Browning, and even that of Shelley and Swinburne, tried, Yeats claimed, 'to absorb into itself the science and politics, the philosophy and morality of its time.'[28] Literature, as the nineteenth century advanced, became utilitarian, rhetorical, sentimental, and journalistic: it turned to study and mimesis of the external world, to commentary on the social, humanitarian, and topical interests of the time, to moral judgement and accusation. English literature, in short, turned into a criticism of life, and began to use as its means of expression the weapons of science: observation, explanation, argument, theory, and erudition.

VI

The writers of the Celtic Revival maintained that the development of Irish literature and history and character was distinct and separate from the development of the English, that the Celtic perception of life was different from the English, and that the Irish people constituted a nation with a distinctive cultural and spiritual heritage. Indeed, so deep was the antagonism between Ireland and England that it sprang, AE claims, from 'biological and spiritual necessity.'[29] This antagonism had expressed itself throughout the centuries in rebellion after rebellion, and the leaders of these rebellions were, AE contends, not merely fighting for a political change, but were the 'desperate and despairing champions of a culture which . . . was being stifled from infancy.'[30] But no amount of physical force or oppression can, AE argues in his seminal

48

pamphlet, *The Inner and The Outer Ireland*, kill the desire to express a national spirit, and so the Irish nation had hung on for centuries, waiting patiently for circumstance to enable them to escape their conquerors, or for the mills of God to grind the British Empire to dust, as other empires had been ground to dust before. This desire to express the national character in literature and in life may seem at times a hopeless cause, but physical death, AE argues in 1901, is preferable to spiritual defeat, or to the denial of the spirit that animates a nation: 'God gives no second gift to a nation if it flings away its birthright. We cannot put on the ideals of another people as a garment.'[31]

At the root, then, of the antagonism between Ireland and England, of the historical rebellions and the literary Revival, was the battle between two traditions, two ways of perceiving the world: 'What is this nationality we are trying to preserve,' Yeats asks in a public lecture in 1903, 'this thing we are fighting English influence to preserve? It is not merely our pride. It is certainly not any national vanity that stirs us on to activity. If you examine to the root a contest between two peoples, two nations, you will always find that it is really a war between two civilizations, two ideals of life.'[32] What the writers of the Celtic Revival were demanding was the freedom to express the 'spiritual life' of the Irish race, the right to work out the national destiny,[33] and to manifest the national genius in a civilization that was not an echo or an imitation of another: 'We ask,' AE pleads, 'the liberty of shaping the social order in Ireland to reflect our own ideals, and to embody that national soul which has been slowly incarnating in our race from its cloudy dawn.'[34] On the outcome of this battle there was more at stake than the destiny of Ireland: the battle was not merely one of Ireland against England, not even one of people against people, but of the individual soul against bureaucracy, of spiritual forces against the forces of empire and state,[35] and a portion of the 'everlasting battle' between light and darkness, good and evil, spirit and matter.[36] In the resolution of this battle, AE contends, lies the hope of humanity, the realization of 'universal human hopes,' the solution of 'eternal problems': the 'typical humanity' of the world, AE writes, 'exists in germ in the spiritual and intellectual outcasts of our time, who can find no place in the present social order.'[37]

VII

The Celtic Revival was deliberately created as a counter-movement to the materialism of the post-Darwinian age. Yeats and AE did not believe in evolution or progress: for these poets, change in the history of man was not slow and methodical, but sudden and miraculous, a leap of the imagination: 'all life is revelation,' Yeats writes, 'beginning in miracle and enthusiasm, and dying out as it unfolds itself in what we have mistaken for progress.'[38] Neither did they believe that literature was a criticism of visible life, but that it was a revelation of an invisible world. They saw the poet not as the servant of society, nor as a passive commentator on the political or social concerns of the time, but as the medium of immortal emotion, writing out of a deeper life than his own, receiving his inspiration from the collective memory of his race, interpreting and remaking the modern world according to the impulses he receives in meditation and vision. 'Talk to me of originality and I will turn on you with rage. I am a crowd, I am a lonely man, I am nothing,' Yeats writes at the end of his life.[39] With Plato and Plotinus, Yeats and AE believed that individual human life was an ephemeral flower blooming from the perennial rhizome, with death returning to the great ocean of being, withering and descending into the rhizome, to bloom again in another spring, in another incarnation. Mankind is not complete, the initiator of action, but merely the foam upon the deep, merely the momentary blossom of some spiritual impulse. Through man, and more particularly through the poet, the invisible moods of the universe work their will; the great unchanging myths are constantly being enacted and re-enacted. The images that present themselves to the poet, therefore, do not originate in his individual consciousness, but are given to him from the composite mind and living memory of his race. They come, as it were, 'out of the ancestral being,' and are more easily apprehended in places where the traditional order of life remains unbroken.[40] This visionary communion of the individual personality and the racial memory, of the modern Irish poet and the Celtic past, Yeats and AE considered as an aspect of the Celtic approach to experience, and over and over in their work they probe the nature and significance of vision, meditation, dream, intuition, imagination, and magic.

In the beginning of the world, and in places where the plough of modern civilization had not cut too deep, as in the Celtic world, there was no separation between matter and spirit: when 'a man beheld a natural object the spiritual thing it expressed came at once into his mind.'[41] All of the material forms of nature were holy and haunted. But as the centuries progressed, mind and matter, the inner spiritual meaning and the outer material form, began to separate, and man turned from the expression of his own mind to the study of the external world for its own sake. Yeats and AE, on the other hand, viewed the world symbolically, seeing the visible material world as the means by which an invisible spiritual essence becomes manifest to mortal eyes, and interpreting all physical and intellectual forms, all art and nature, as the expression or embodiment of the universal mood at the centre of the universe which Yeats calls God.[42] Materialism, according to Yeats, reaches its high-water mark during the twentieth century, but at this point, suddenly, miraculously, the opposite of all that is characteristic of materialistic thought is born. Man, having become enchanted with the outer form, to possessions and the consequences of action, suddenly becomes sated with science, sensation, and analyses of the external world, and he returns instinctively and dramatically to the spiritual world he has neglected. Yeats links the Celtic Revival to this symbolic apocalypse that was to sweep away the concept of literature as a criticism of life and to usher in 'an age of imagination, of emotion, of moods, of revelation.'[43] 'This revolution,' Yeats writes, 'may be the opportunity for the Irish Celt, for he has an unexhausted and inexhaustible mythology to give him symbols and personages, and his nature has been profoundly emotional from the beginning.'[44]

VIII

Rejecting the earlier traditions of Irish writing in English – the tradition of Congreve, Goldsmith, Sheridan, and their followers, who used England and London as a platform for the expression of Irish wit and anarchical wisdom; the tradition of Edmund Burke and Bernard Shaw who, starting from the premise that Ireland was an integral part of the United Kingdom, believed that the moral purification of England and the Empire could be accomplished by Irishmen; and the tradition of the Young Ireland writers, who created 'images for the affections' of the Irish people by using

English literary models[45] – rejecting these traditions, the writers of the Celtic Revival turned to poetry in the Irish language, to folklore, and to myth.

Yeats was interested in Gaelic poetry because of the natural energies it celebrated, because it was not a poetry of material security, success, and complacence, but a poetry articulating the beliefs and hopes of the weak and vulnerable, and, like the poetry of the Rhymers' Club, created out of the despair and desolation of defeat. The fact that it was a poetry built on dreams linked it in Yeats's mind to the nature of all great poetry:

> Poetry is the utterance of desires that we can only satisfy in dreams, and . . . if all our dreams were satisfied there would be no more poetry. . . . The children of the poor and simple learn from their unbroken religious faith, and from their traditional beliefs, and from the hardness of their lives, that this world is nothing, and that a spiritual world, where all dreams come true, is everything; and therefore the poor and simple are that imperfection whose perfection is genius.[46]

In their collections of folklore and in their work based on folklore, Yeats, Lady Gregory, Douglas Hyde, and John Synge discovered or created an approach to life that contravened the modern materialistic approach. Ireland, they maintained, was one of the last spiritual strongholds in Europe, and the Celt, they held, still retained contact with the mystery and imagination that existed before man fell a slave to the external world. In Celtic folklore, too, Yeats and AE found corroboration for their occult experiments and philosophic reading: evidence of the existence of an invisible world, of the continuance of life after death, and proof of the immortality of the soul.[47]

The Celt, in the stories collected or created by the writers of the Revival, is not concerned with probability or necessity, but only with the expression of emotion. He perceives the correspondence between sensuous form and supersensuous meaning and recognizes instinctively the spirit that gives a voice to the dumb things that surround him. Not distinguishing clearly between the natural and the supernatural, and believing that all nature is full of invisible spirits that can be perceived by those willing to look beyond the cobweb veil of the senses, the Celt sees everything as enchanted. He is filled with reverence for the past and a sense of the sanctity and mystery of everything that surrounds him. The mythical associations of topographical sites are fresh in his mind. To the Celt in these stories, the land is still holy and haunted.

The Celt, the writers of the Revival found, did not live in a shrunken over-defined world, but lingered constantly 'on the edges of vision,' learning to live with the spirits that haunted his solitary world, seeking to capture in imagination, idiom or tale 'some high, impalpable mood,' attempting to express 'a something that lies beyond the range of expression'[48] creating, like the Rhymers, in the deprivation of material life, a mask or compensating dream. Like great artists, these visionaries had the power to mythologize places and people, to transform mortal men and women into the immortal images of art, to transform, for example, Mary Hynes and Raftery into 'perfect symbols of the sorrow of beauty and of the magnificence and penury of dreams.'[49] And like great artists, these Celtic visionaries possessed a living permanent tradition that refused to surrender to the 'small arrogant oligarchy' of those who merely happen to be walking around; they possessed traditional images and emotions that carried 'their memories backward thousands of years.'[50] They communed with the dead generations, receiving from the racial memory images that come to meditative minds. They were fully cognizant of the tragedy and imperfections of unaccommodated man, realizing the brevity of life, accepting the conditions of life, and summoning courage and dignity when faced with defeat and death.

Alone among European nations, Ireland, Yeats claimed, possessed a wealth of folk stories and legends that had not yet been shaped into modern literature:

> Ireland has in her written Gaelic literature, in her old love tales and battle tales, the forms in which the imagination of Europe uttered itself before Greece shaped a tumult of legend into the music of her arts; and she can discover, from the beliefs and emotions of her common people, the habit of mind that created the religion of the muses. The legends of other European countries are less numerous, and not so full of the energies from which the arts and our understanding of their sanctity arose, and the best of them have already been shaped into plays and poems.[51]

The aim of the leaders of the Celtic Revival was to combine the imagination that is expressed in folklore and legend with the imagination that has produced the wrought sophisticated literature of the world, in other words to bridge the written and unwritten traditions and to establish a modern literary tradition on emotions that came from the heart of the people. The artist, they argued, must realize that he is the spiritual leader of his people, and he must adopt the 'method and the fervour of a priesthood.'[52] Like the priest, he must root his art in ancient ceremonies and use them to illuminate and interpret the unchanging passions of daily life. The scientific movement had pushed modern literature into one of two directions: into subservience to an external reality or a concern with rarefied essences. One type of literature was concerned with the spiritual element which the other type denied, but neglected the interest in common life with which the other literature was too much concerned.[53] We remember Synge's famous stricture of both types in the Preface to *The Playboy of the Western World*, of the literature of Mallarmé on the one hand, and the literature of Ibsen on the other. The Celtic Literary Revival aimed at the reconciliation of art and life, imagination and reality, the spiritual and the common, the seen and the unseen. The modern Irish poet, these writers maintained, must learn what the common people knew instinctively: sanctity of place, a sense of tradition, love of the unseen, the daring and imaginative impulse that animates folk life and legend.

IX

When we turn from folklore to myth and to the problems in creating a modern literature out of old myths, we find ourselves on a more difficult terrain. The scientific explanation of the phenomenal world, separating as it did the intellect from emotion and the imagination, did not satisfy the whole being, and left the senses cold. We can trace the horror of the poet caught in a scientific age without the resources of myth in two of the characteristic poems produced in England during the nineteenth and twentieth centuries, *In Memoriam* and *The Waste Land*. Myth is created by the imagination acting on the evidence of the senses and is a prerational attempt to explain human life and the universe. Since, as Professor Lorna Reynolds argues, the new areas of human experience that Yeats and his fellow-writers were elucidating were part of the subconscious deposit of the pre-rational development of man, they turned instinctively to myth.[54] Myth is sensuous and concrete: it explains and dramatizes events in the external world in terms of the 'unconscious drama' of the human psyche:[55] the adventures of mythic heroes, AE explains, may 'correspond to adventures of the spirit, conflicts between the bright power and the dark powers in ourselves.'[56] Without a traditional mythology, a writer must rely on the inventiveness of his own mind; his creations, consequently, must be arbitrary and original. Through myth, on the other hand, an artist is brought beyond the limitations of his individual being, beyond the accidental forms of the world to the essence that these forms embody and to the imaginative events and characters in which these essences were first expressed in the national consciousness. A modern man living without myth is, Jung writes, 'like one uprooted, having no true link either with the past, or with the ancestral life which continues within him, or yet with contemporary human society. He . . . lives a life of his own, sunk in a subjective mania of his own devising, which he believes to be the newly discovered truth.'[57] Myth provides an extravagant expression of pure emotion – of love, terror, joy, friendship – a means of re-shaping the world according to the impulses and desires of the human psyche, working in communion with the collective memory of the race, and without any regard to prudence, practicality, probability, or necessity.[58] It deals with imaginative events and characters which, having been brooded upon by generations and tested throughout the centuries, are 'steeped in emotion,'[59] characters and events created at a time when 'the elemental virtues' were prized[60] and which have been brought to a kind of perfection because they are not the work of one mind but of many minds (the same feature, incidentally, that attracted Yeats to Byzantine mosaics). With myth, therefore, and a literature created from myth, modern man is released from the despair of an industrialized Iron age, and is provided with a link between his own age and the heroic age of the past, between his own individual consciousness and the consciousness of his race.

A race does not change in essentials: only the circumstances of life change. What was embodied in the Celtic mythic heroes may, AE argues, still be natural and innate in the character of the race. Cuchulain, AE goes on to suggest, must be restored to the

twentieth-century consciousness at the precise point when the
modern Irish nation was beginning to form, because he embodies
'all that the bards thought noblest in the spirit of their race.'[61]
Myth is concerned with the heroic, and in their work the writers
of the Celtic Revival consciously created for the popular mind
heroic models of human behaviour and encouraged the nation to
emulate these models through all the vicissitudes of earthly life.[62]
One does not have to search deeply in Yeats's work to discover
what he thought characteristic of the heroic approach to life: self-
possession, acceptance of the conditions of life, abandonment to
impulse and emotion, to whatever impulse is most immediate and
pressing, courage when confronted with impossible odds, gaiety in
the face of terror and defeat, indifference to death. One should also
consider in this context the way in which Yeats contributes to the
imaginative entity that we have called a nation by celebrating or
mythologizing the heroic acts and character of his contemporaries,
the gallery of living presences he creates in his poetry by releasing
his contemporaries from cold history and time, capturing each in
his most characteristic pose, making out of mortal men and women
symbols to be brooded over in the coming times: Maud Gonne,
Roger Casement, Patrick Pearse, The O'Rahilly, John Synge, John
Butler Yeats, Robert Gregory, MacGregor Mathers, and many
others.

Myths are also connected with places that men still inhabit,
places sanctified by the passions enacted there in ancient times,
and which still retain emotional residues of that passion: 'in our
land,' Yeats writes,

> there is no river or mountain that is not associated in the memory
> with some event or legend. . . . I would have our writers and
> craftsmen of many kinds master this history and these legends,
> and fix upon their memory the appearance of mountains and
> rivers and make it all visible again in their arts, so that Irishmen,
> even though they had gone thousands of miles away, would still
> be in their own country. . . . I would have Ireland re-create the
> ancient arts, the arts as they were understood . . . in every ancient
> land; as they were understood when they moved a whole people
> and not a few people who had grown up in a leisured class and
> made this understanding their business. . . . I would have . . .
> [scholars and artists] begin to dig in Ireland the garden of the

future, understanding that here in Ireland the spirit of man may be about to wed the soil of the world.[63]

By rooting his art in places with mythic associations, an artist makes his country live in the imagination of his own people and in the imagination of the world. We are familiar with the way in which Yeats mythologizes places in many of his poems, capturing the light and colour of the Irish climate and scenery, restoring to places their mythological associations, and giving them new levels of poetic association,[64] while some of his plays – *The Dreaming of the Bones, The Words Upon the Window-Pane*, and *Purgatory* – derive their dramatic strength from being set in places where human passions played out in ancient times prove more powerful than the presence of the living.

X

'In a little time,' Yeats writes, 'places may begin to seem the only hieroglyphs that cannot be forgotten, and poets . . . will come . . . nearer the old poets, who had a seat at every hearth, if they but mingle their own dream with a story told for centuries.'[65] What the writers of the Celtic Revival attempted to do was to knead the qualities that animate myth and folk literature into the circumstances of the life of an Irish artist living in the twentieth century, to produce a literature that retained the idealism of country people without 'renouncing the complexity of ideas and emotions which is the heritage of cultivated man.'[66] We may cite a few examples from Yeats's work to indicate how he used myth to dramatize moments or situations that have become or are becoming part of the twentieth-century approach to experience: the juxtaposition of intense vision and orthodox concerns which forms part of the art of the 1937 *Vision, Ideas of Good and Evil*, and the occult stories he produced during the eighteen-nineties. In *The King's Threshold*, the hunger strike is, I gather, used for the first time in life or in literature to gain a personal or political objective. Deirdre, Yeats makes symbolic of twentieth-century woman and of woman's liberation from domestic and sexual enslavement, of her right to choose her fate, and having chosen it, to face heroically the consequences of that choice: Deirdre, Yeats writes, 'might be some mild housewife but for her prophetic wisdom.'[67] *On Baile's Strand*, a play filled with emotion of multitude, is one of the first plays of the absurd, where we have a true juxtaposition of incongruities: of the spiritual and the common, the Golden Age and the Iron Age, [68] the heroic impulse and the material betrayal of that impulse, all caught in one movement at the end of the play.

In rooting his art in myth, the artist, Yeats suggests, may be responding to impulses which 'have been accumulating for centuries,'[69] but once he has chosen his subject he must be concerned with nothing further than the expression of his own personality: he must, in Yeats's words, 'think of nothing but giving it [his subject] such an expression as will please himself. . . . He must make his work a part of his own journey towards beauty and truth.'[70] Personality is the expression of the energy that is unique to an individual engaged in active life or literature,[71] an expression unmotivated by ulterior advantage, material advancement, or that 'last infirmity of Noble mind,' what John Milton calls 'Fame.' Personality is the living personal element that animates action, language, and thought. It is what makes one man's perception of the world different from another, originating in the uniqueness of each individual, and expressing itself in action or in a work of art with an energy that remains after the dictates of logic and necessity have been satisfied.[72] Initially the artist's vision may seem at variance with his countrymen's preconceptions, for he presents his images as he sees them, not as his people expect him to see them.[73] The battle between the artist and his audience, and Yeats's defence of the right of the artist, whether he be a Synge or an O'Casey, to embody his own vision without regard to any utilitarian or obviously nationalistic cause, could be traced in another paper.[74] A national literature, Yeats writes, is created by writers 'who are moulded by influences that are moulding their country, and who write out of so deep a life that they are accepted there in the end.'[75] And in *A Portrait of the Artist as a Young Man* Joyce writes: 'This race and this country and this life produced me. . . . I shall express myself as I am.'[76] By expressing his own personality, an artist inevitably expresses the deeper thoughts and emotions of his race. To be national is to be personal.

XI

Out of the confluence, therefore, of space, place, personality, and gifted Irish writers, the Celtic Literary Revival was created. It is important to realize that the Revival is the modern culmination or blossom of an ancient tradition, the roots of which run deeper than the events that have shaped the western world. The literature of the Celtic Revival must be approached in the context out of which it was created: it cannot properly be understood without a knowledge of the Celtic background, of the people, history, language, folklore and myths of the Celtic race. To approach it in any other way, as a side branch of English literature, for example, is as misguided and as unscholarly as to teach Irish history as a branch of British colonial history.

XII

Since much of what I have said involves politics and literature, I shall conclude with a brief exploration of the relation between the two. The economist Maynard Keynes writes: 'The political fanatic who is hearing voices in the air has distilled his frenzy from the work of some academic scribbler of a few years back.'[77] When we are dealing not merely with an 'academic scribbler' but with a community of great artists, the voice that stirs the fanatic to political activity may be irresistible. The language that Yeats and AE use to advocate cultural and political separation from Britain was as uncompromising and as calculated to stir the soul of the nation as the language of Patrick Pearse, James Connolly, and their revolutionary associates. In *The National Being*, published in 1916, AE writes:

> When national ideals have been created they assume an immeasurably greater dignity when the citizens organize themselves for the defence of their ideals, and are prepared to yield up life itself as a sacrifice if by this the national being may be preserved. . . . There are occasions when the manhood of a nation must be prepared to yield life rather than submit to oppression, when it must perish in self-contempt or resist by force what wrong would be imposed by force. . . . We are standing on the threshold of nationhood.[78]

Earlier, in 1903, a year after the stirring production of *Cathleen Ni Houlihan* with Maud Gonne playing the lead, Yeats stated in a public lecture which is as yet unpublished:

59

When I speak to myself those names that are rated upon the rosary of our national life; when I repeat to myself the name of Parnell, that haughty and austere spirit, or the name of Wolfe Tone, that joyful spirit, who kept his triumph and [triumphant?] air even under the shadow of death; when I think of the Red Man of the O'Donnells and of that Hugh O'Neill, who seemed, even when a lad, to be born to be a prince of men, who was born, the chronicler said, for the great weal or woe of his country; when I think of those men I say to myself that the greatest sin a man can commit against his race and against mankind is to bring the work of the dead to nothing. . . . We all hope that Ireland's battle is drawing to an end, but we must live as though it were to go on endlessly. We must . . . pass on into the future the great moral qualities that give men the strength to fight. . . . It may be that it depends upon us to call into life the phantom armies of the future. If we keep that thought always before us, if we never allow ourselves to forget those armies, we need have no fear for the future of Ireland.[79]

Through the power of the imagination of the leaders of the Celtic Revival, Cuchulain, a Bronze Age hero, suddenly re-appears in the twentieth century, and he appears not only in literary works, but he becomes a living image and presence, a model for the expression of the heroic impulse. Cuchulain provides the inspiration for one of the most significant historical events in the twentieth century, the Easter Rising of 1916, which was itself conceived and enacted as a theatrical event,[80] and which heralded the break-up of the mightiest empire ever forged in the history of the world. When facing the might of the British Empire in an insurrection that had no possibility of succeeding in the way that we understand success, the insurgents were conscious of the spirit of Cuchulain when he too faced impossible odds: Pearse and his companions imagined themselves as sacrificial heroes and gave up their lives not only to free their country, but to demonstrate that heroes still could be found in the modern world:

When Pearse summoned Cuchulain to his side,
What stalked through the Post Office? What intellect,
What calculation, number, measurement, replied?[81]

The figures of mythology are created early in the life of a nation, and not only continue to live in people's imaginations, but are embodied in each generation.[82] It was the power of the literary interpretations of the figures of myth that led to the creation of the state of modern Ireland:

> What was in Patrick Pearse's soul when he fought in Easter Week [AE asks] but an imagination, and the chief imagination which inspired him was that of a hero who stood against a host. . . . I who knew how deep was Pearse's love for the Cuchulain whom O'Grady discovered or invented, remembered after Easter Week that he had been solitary against a great host in imagination with Cuchulain, long before circumstance permitted him to stand for his nation with so few companions against so great a power.[83]

In any movement the artists come first. They are the antennae of the nation, picking up impulses before they are perceived by the poor, loveless, ever-anxious crowd. AE states clearly:

> It was our literature more than our political activities which created . . . a true image of our nationality, and brought about the recognition of a spiritual entity which should have a political body to act through.[84]

After the artists come the politicians and parliamentarians who create a physical body for the spiritual and intellectual ideals, then finally the murderous mob who repeat what once was a discovery until it becomes a dead cliché, a hollow and meaningless formula:

> We pieced our thoughts into philosophy,
> And planned to bring the world under a rule,
> Who are but weasels fighting in a hole.[85]

Robert O'Driscoll

ACKNOWLEDGEMENT. I wish to express my gratitude to Bill and Cathy Graham and to Mr and Mrs Hugh Curry for a log-cabin and a portion of Glenariff Farm, Ontario, where this paper was written.

NOTES

1   John Pinkerton, *An Enquiry into the History of Scotland* (London, 1789), II, 18-19.
2   *History of Ireland: Heroic Period,* I (London, 1878), p. v.
3   *Uncollected Prose of W. B. Yeats,* ed. John Frayne, I (London: Macmillan, 1970), p. 368.
4   AE, 'Nationality and Imperialism,' in *Ideals of Ireland,* ed. Lady Gregory (London: Unicorn Press, 1901), p. 15.
5   *Uncollected Prose,* p. 348.
6   *Essays and Introductions* (London: Macmillan, 1961), p. 111. Subsequent references to this volume will be abbreviated to *E & I.*
7   *The Living Torch,* ed. Monk Gibbon (London: Macmillan, 1937), p. 134.
8   *Ibid.,* p. 183.
9   *Uncollected Prose,* p. 273.
10 *The Living Torch,* p. 135.
11 *Idem.*
12 *Ibid.,* p. 184.
13 *Ibid.,* p. 259.
14 *Ibid.,* p. 197.
15 *Ibid.,* p. 263.
16 *Ibid.,* p. 135.
17 *The National Being* (Dublin: Maunsel, 1916), p. 12.
18 *Ideals in Ireland,* p. 15.
19 *E & I,* pp. 513-4.
20 *The Revival of Irish Literature,* ed. Charles Gavan Duffy (London: Unwin, 1894), pp. 124-6.
21 'It is possible to argue', AE writes, that Shakespeare's imagination of Henry V was 'the first imperial mood in English literature and the begetter in millions of men's minds of like moods' (*Living Torch,* p. 135). Yeats, also, comments on the part that Shakespeare's imagination of Henry V played in the shaping of the imperialistic consciousness (see *E & I,* pp. 104-5).
22 The growth of cities, AE argues, cuts the cord that connects man to Nature, the Great Mother: 'life shrivels up, sundered from the source of life. . . . [I]n the cities there is a slow poisoning of life going on day by day. . . . It is only in Nature, and by thoughts on the problems of Nature, that our intellect grows to any real truth and draws near to the Mighty Mind which laid the foundations of the world' (*National Being,* pp. 62-3). Yeats also argues that life in cities 'deafens or kills the passive meditative life', and that modern education merely

'enlarges the separated, self-moving mind' and makes our souls less sensitive to supernatural influences (*E & I*, p. 41).

23 AE, *Thoughts for a Convention* (Dublin and London, 1917), p. 10.
24 *Ibid.*, p. 7. AE wrote these words after the 1916 Rising, but he had made the same point several times earlier in his writings. The rejection of the imperialist ideal is the recurring theme of an important, but often over-looked book, *Ideals in Ireland*, edited by Lady Gregory in 1900, which contains contributions by Yeats, AE, Douglas Hyde, George Moore, Standish O'Grady and D. P. Moran (see especially pp. 19-20, p. 50 and p. 106).
25 *E & I*, p. 109.
26 *Ibid.*, p. 114. In *Literary Ideals in Ireland* (Dublin: Daily Express, 1899), Yeats writes: 'Modern poetry grows weary of using over and over again the personages and stories and metaphors that have come to us through Greece and Rome, or from Wales and Brittany through the Middle ages. . . . The Irish legends, in popular tradition and in old Gaelic literature, are . . . numerous, and . . . alone among great European legends have the beauty and wonder of altogether new things' (pp. 18-9).
27 *Explorations*, ed. Mrs. W. B. Yeats (London: Macmillan, 1962), p. 205.
28 *E & I*, p. 190.
29 *The Inner and The Outer Ireland* (Dublin: Talbot Press, 1921), p. 5.
30 *Thoughts for a Convention*, p. 6.
31 *Ideals in Ireland*, p. 20.
32 Unpublished Lecture in the possession of Senator Michael Yeats.
33 AE writes: 'If the universe has any meaning at all it exists for the purposes of soul, and men or nations denied essential freedom cannot fulfil their destiny, or illuminate earth with light or wisdom from that divinity without them, or mould external circumstance into the image of the Heaven they conceive in their hearts' (*The Inner and The Outer Ireland*, p. 15).
34 *Ideals in Ireland*, p. 18. In the same collection of essays, D. P. Moran writes: A literature steeped in the history, traditions, and genius of one nation is at best only an imperfect tutor to the people of another nation" (p. 31).
35 On this point AE writes: 'The battle which is going on in the world has been stated to be a spiritual conflict between those who desire greater freedom for the individual and think that the state exists to preserve that freedom, and those who believe in the predominance of the state and the complete subjection of the individual to it and the moulding of the individual mind in its image' (*Thoughts for a Convention*, p. 27).
36 AE writes: The 'struggle is in reality not against flesh and blood, but is a portion of the everlasting battle against principalities and powers and spiritual wickedness in high places, which underlies every other battle which has been or will be fought by men' (*Ideals in Ireland*, p. 21).
37 *Ideals in Ireland*, p. 17. See also p. 22.
38 *E & I*, p. 171.

39 *Ibid.*, p. 522.

40 *Ibid.*, p. 36 and p. 42. In his essay on 'Magic' Yeats argues that the images which present themselves to the poet from a deeper life than his own bear a 'definite relation to dominant moods and moulding events' of his own age. When the poet looks beyond the external and the superficial, however, these images or visions seem 'symbolical histories of these moods and events, or rather symbolical shadows of the impulses that have made them' (*E & I*, p. 36).

41 Yeats and Ellis, *The Works of William Blake*, 3 vols. (London: Quaritch, 1893), I, 291.

42 *Ibid.*, pp. 241-2. See also my Dolmen monograph, *Symbolism and Some Implications of the Symbolic Approach: W. B. Yeats during the Eighteen-Nineties* (Dublin, 1975), pp. 10-19.

43 *E & I*, p. 197.

44 *Uncollected Prose*, p. 377.

45 *Explorations*, p. 313.

46 *Ideals in Ireland*, p. 94.

47 In *Visions and Beliefs in the West of Ireland*, Lady Gregory writes:
> If by an impossible miracle every trace and memory of Christianity could be swept out of the world, it would not shake or destroy at all the belief of the people in Ireland in the invisible world, the cloud of witnesses, in immortality and the life to come. For them the veil between things seen and unseen has hardly thickened since those early days of the world. . . . Here in Connacht there is no doubt as to the continuance of life after death (New York: Oxford University Press, Gerrards Cross: Colin Smythe, 1970, p. 190).

48 *The Celtic Twilight* (1893), pp. 24-5 and p. 20. For the earlier quotation in this sentence, see *E & I*, p. 42.

49 *Mythologies*, p. 30.

50 *E & I*, p. 6.

51 *Ideals in Ireland*, p. 98.

52 *E & I*, p. 203.

53 In his essays on 'The Irish Dramatic Movement', published in *Explorations*, Yeats explores this question at length. See pp. 149-50, 163, 167, 185.

54 'Response to the Assessors', one of the documents which formed part of the *Yeats Studies* Application to the Canada Council (1975-6), as yet unpublished.

55 *The Basic Writings of C. G. Jung*, ed. Violet Staub De Laszlo (New York: Random House, 1959), p. 289.

56 *The Living Torch*, p. 244.

57 *Basic Writings*, p. 5.

58 Yeats writes:
> Its events, and things, and people are wild, and are like unbroken horses, that are so much more beautiful than horses that have learned to run between shafts. . . . The great virtues, the great joys, the great privations come in the myths, and, as it were, take mankind between their naked arms, and without putting off their divinity. Poets have taken their themes more often from stories that are all, or half,

mythological, than from history or stories that give one the sensation of history, understanding, as I think, that the imagination which remembers the proportions of life is but a long wooing, and that it has to forget them before it becomes the torch and the marriage-bed (*Explorations*, p. 10).

59 *E & I*, p. 114.

60 *The Living Torch*, p. 240. AE writes:

As that extraordinary bardic literature, so much richer in imagination than the ballad poetry which influenced Scott, becomes more widely known, may we not hope Irish writers of genius will see in its legendary heroes and demigods the noblest symbols of their own emotions? That bardic literature was written at a time when little was prized except the elemental virtues, and the study of it excites the spirit in an age of complex thought, when people are praised for scientific attainment or intellect (*The Living Torch*, pp. 239-40).

61 *The National Being*, p. 12.

62 'Our political life in the past,' AE writes, 'has been sordid and unstable because we were uncultured as a nation. National ideals have been the possession of the few in Ireland, and have not been diffused. That is the cause of our comparative failure as a nation. If we would create an Irish culture, and spread it widely among our people, we would have the same unfathomable sources of inspiration and sacrifice to draw upon in our acts as a nation as the individual has who believes he is immortal, and that his life here is but a temporary foray into time out of eternity' (*The National Being*, p. 136).

63 *Essays and Introductions*, pp. 205-10. Yeats makes this point several times throughout his work. In *Literary Ideals in Ireland* he writes:

Our legends are always associated with places, and not merely every mountain and valley, but every strange stone and little coppice has its legend, preserved in written or unwritten tradition. Our Irish Romantic movement has arisen out of this tradition, and should always, even when it makes new legends about traditional people and things, be haunted by places. It should make Ireland, as Ireland and all other lands were in ancient times, a holy land to her own people (pp. 19-20).

Every lake and mountain in the land where a people live must, Yeats writes in *Ideas of Good and Evil*, be made 'an excitement of the imagination" (*E & I*, p. 209). And in *The Cutting of An Agate*, Yeats writes:

Until the discovery of legendary knowledge and the returning belief in miracle, or what we must needs call so, can bring once more a new belief in the sanctity of common ploughland, and new wonders that reward no difficult ecclesiastical routine but the common, wayward, spirited man, we may never see again a Shelley and a Dickens in the one body. . . . I am orthodox and pray for a resurrection of the body, and am certain that a man should find his Holy Land where he first crept upon the floor, and that familiar woods and rivers should fade into symbol with so gradual a change that he may never discover, no, not even in ecstasy itself, that he is

65

beyond space, and that time alone keeps him from Primum Mobile, Supernal Eden, Yellow Rose over all (*E & I*, pp. 296-97).

64 Yeats writes: 'I sought some symbolic language reaching far into the past and associated with familiar name and conspicuous hills that I might not be alone amid the obscure impressions of the senses' (*E & I*, p. 349).

65 *Ideals in Ireland*, p. 100.

66 *Ibid.*, p. 91. AE maintains that the Celtic Revival, which was an assertion of the 'spiritual personality' of Ireland, produced a literature that was both ancient and modern, ancient because it was rooted in the 'almost forgotten fountain of Gaelic culture,' and at the same time 'intensely modern' in that it had 'enough of the universal in it to win recognition from lovers of literature in Europe and America' (*The Living Torch*, p. 247).

67 *Explorations*, p. 11.

68 With myth, and a literature created from myth, Yeats and AE argue, we have a sense of the Golden Age balancing the Modern age. Yeats writes: 'romantic art is . . . about to change its manner and become more like the art of the old poets, who saw the golden age and their own age side by side like substance and shadow' (*Ideals in Ireland*, p. 99). AE claims that with myth we 'feel . . . that we are travelling in the realms of gold . . . the Golden Age has never passed away but is always about us, and it is a vision which can be regained by any who will light some of the candles in the many mansions of the spirit' (*The Living Torch*, 240-2).

69 *Uncollected Prose*, p. 360.

70 *E & I*, pp. 206-7.

71 'I have always come to this certainty,' Yeats writes in 1906, 'what moves natural men in the arts is what moves them in life, and that is, intensity of personal life, intonations that show them, in a book or a play, the strength, the essential moment of a man who would be exciting in the market or at the dispensary door' (*E & I*, p. 265).

72 See *E & I*, pp. 253 ff. See also my essay, 'Yeats's Conception of Synge,' in *Sunshine and the Moon's Delight: A Centenary Tribute to John Millington Synge 1871-1909*, ed. S. B. Bushrui (Gerrards Cross, Bucks: Smythe, 1972), pp. 159-71, and my essay, 'Yeats on Personality: Three Unpublished Lectures,' in *Yeats and the Theatre*, edd. Robert O'Driscoll and Lorna Reynolds (Toronto: Macmillan, 1975), pp. 4-59.

73 See the 'Introduction' to my *Theatre and Nationalism in Twentieth-Century Ireland* (Toronto: University of Toronto Press; London: Oxford University Press, 1971).

74 Yeats's essays on 'The Irish Dramatic Movement,' published in *Explorations*, pp. 103-60, focus on this problem: the gulf that inevitably develops between national expectations and the artist who has the courage to express his own vision.

75 *Explorations*, p. 156.

76 (London, 1964), pp. 204-5.

77 Quoted in J. R. Talmon, *Political Messianism: Romantic Phase* (New York, 1960), p. 256.

78 *The National Being,* pp. 134-40. AE does go on to argue, however, that moral and economic forces are 'more powerful than physical' ones (p. 153): the 'military and political institutions of a small country are comparatively easy to displace,' but it is a task 'infinitely more difficult to destroy ideals or to extinguish a national being' (p. 135). He advocates the application of the discipline one learns from military training, the sacrifice of the individual for the general welfare, to civil life. AE is, indeed, more interested in the creation of 'intellectual and spiritual armies': 'some time in the heroic future,' he writes, 'some nation in a crisis . . . will oppose moral and spiritual forces to material forces. . . . [N]othing will put an end to race conflicts except the equally determined and heroic development of the spiritual, moral, and intellectual forces which disdain to use the force and fury of material powers' (pp. 154-6).

79 'The Intellectual Revival in Ireland' in the possession of Senator Michael Yeats, pp. 2-17.

80 The theatrical aspects of the Rising are clear in the time and setting chosen for the event, and in the dress, actions, and theatrical concerns of the major participants.

Many of the leaders of the Rising – Pearse, Plunkett, and MacDonagh – were, as we know, poets and playwrights, and perhaps more importantly, they had directed plays. F. X. Martin directs our attention to the conspicuously theatrical element in their very dress and public gestures: MacDonagh with his sword-stick and cloak; Eamonn Ceannt with his kilt and bagpipes; Plunkett with his immense Celtic rings and bracelets, marrying in a midnight ceremony the night before his execution at dawn; the dying Connolly tied to a stretcher to be shot; Countess Markiewicz 'concluding her activities in Easter Week at the time of the surrender by ostentatiously kissing her revolver and Sam Browne belt as she handed them over to the British Officer'; and Pearse himself reading the Proclamation of the Irish Republic with the 'classical front' of the General Post Office and its 'Ionic pillars and portico' serving as a background, and the night before his execution writing the final moving poem to his mother (see F. X. Martin, '1916 – Myth, Fact, and Mystery,' *Studia Hibernica,* No. 7 (Dublin, 1967 [1968]), pp. 10-11).

The theatrical aspect of the Rising was also apparent in the choice of setting, the seizing of the public buildings in Dublin which, although disastrous choices as military headquarters, meant that the insurrection would cut across the routine life of the city. The time chosen for the event was also theatrical: spring and April with the emergence of new life from the dead of winter; and Easter with the traditional religious associations of the Resurrection.

Viewing the Rising from the inside of the Post Office, Michael Collins said that 'it had the air of a Greek tragedy' (Rex Taylor, *Michael Collins,* London 1958, p. 77). The rebels in many ways seemed to have conceived of themselves as characters in a tragedy; in casting themselves in these self-appointed roles, in imagining themselves as sacrificial heroes, they were conscious of re-enacting myth, and when the moment of reckoning .came, as was inevitable, they refused to shirk the responsibility that was involved in living up to the roles that they had chosen.

The Rising was a calculated theatrical gamble and a daring success in that it ignited the political imagination and energy of the country. The survivors of the Rising did not make the military mistakes that the initiators had made, and in their successful achievement of Irish independence they mastered the modern techniques of guerilla warfare, and opened the way in which many other oppressed nations secured their independence. It has been suggested that the three greatest experts on guerilla tactics were Tom Barry, Ché Guevara, and Ho Chi Minh, and Tom Barry's *Guerilla Days in Ireland* was Ché Guevara's bible and source book.

81 Yeats, *Collected Poems*, p. 375. The question that inevitably arises is, of course: why were not Yeats and AE in the Post Office? It is not merely a case of the artist being a contemplative man and the politician being a man of action, but rather a matter of the politician becoming enchanted by the abstraction of his own ideals, while the artist is full of a sense of the complexity and the ever-changing patterns of human life. Yeats explores this in *Easter 1916,* and in *The Living Torch* AE writes: 'The poet always has his heart fixed on life in its fullness, on the complete man, and will not starve life for the sake of the patriotic man, and he is a truer patriot than those who have nothing else but patriotism. Our spiritual, intellectual and economic life, all that is necessary to our humanity and its fullness, has been ravaged by those who have set abstractions above humanity' (p. 167).

82 'They are immortals,' AE writes, 'and find bodies from generation to generation' (*The Living Torch,* p. 134).

83 *The Living Torch,* pp. 134-44.

84 *Ibid.,* p. 247. Elsewhere AE writes: 'The spirit which brought about national independence was a spirit created by the artists in life [i.e. heroes and great men of history], but the poets, the musicians, the architects, and, in some way, those who struggled for freedom were inspired and sustained by thoughts and images created by the artists in life and associated with the national being' (*Ibid.,* p. 184).

85 Yeats, *Collected Poems*, p. 233.

THE PARNELL THEME IN LITERATURE

F. S. L. LYONS

The biographer of Charles Stewart Parnell cannot but be aware of the literary resonances of that famous name. But the moment he turns from what the man did and was in his own lifetime, to what the writers made of him thereafter, he finds himself in a predicament. It is the predicament of a student trained to deal with what passes for historical reality who not only has to adjust himself to the existence of something loosely defined as myth, but has to recognise also that myth can itself be a kind of historical reality. Where Parnell is concerned, there is indeed no difficulty in recognising either the existence of the myth or its impact upon history, but the tasks of definition and analysis are greatly complicated by two unusual features of the case. The first is that because of the circumstances of his career, and because of the course of events in the decades after his death, the myth was both powerful and Protean; it not only spread its influence in many directions, but changed its character according to the needs of the individuals who used it, and according to the exigencies of the situations with which they had to grapple. The second unusual feature of the case is that the historical reality with which the myth has to be compared has proved extraordinarily resistant to investigation. Although Parnell was easily the most outstanding Irish leader of the second half of the nineteenth century, the gap between the immensity of his fame and the paucity of the materials available to document that fame is so great that it may never be possible to know him in the sense that, say, O'Connell or de Valera can be known. Yet, while some of his essence will probably always escape us, the researches of the last twenty years have enabled us to construct a Parnell significantly different from the Parnell who inspired the myth. We shall have to look at this discrepancy in due course, but first the myth itself must be identified.

The obvious point of departure is that feature of Parnell's career upon which all commentators are agreed – the personal domination he exercised over his contemporaries. As has often been pointed out, the very qualities that separated him from the people he led were also the qualities that set him above them and so seemed to give a special sanction to his authority – that he was an Anglo-Irish Protestant landlord; that he was a proud man who held his followers at a distance; that he practised silence, not rhetoric; that he curbed passion with rigid self-control; even that he expressed his hatred of England in the impeccable accent of the English governing-class.

To all outward appearances this domination remained absolute until that day in December 1889 when Captain O'Shea filed suit to divorce his wife Katharine for adultery, citing Parnell as co-respondent. We shall see presently that Parnell's mastery over his party and his political environment was not nearly so complete as was supposed at the time. Nevertheless, the contrast between his seeming inviolability and what actually happened when, after bitter debate in Committee Room Fifteen of the House of Commons, a majority of his followers repudiated him under pressure from the English Liberal party which could not stomach a divorcee as the potential head of a future Irish government, was profoundly shocking to Irish opinion. This traumatic experience was still further intensified when the bitter warfare of the succeeding months was ended by his death in October 1891 at the age of forty-five.

The extreme savagery of that final struggle, its abrupt and terrible conclusion, the extraordinary scenes at Parnell's funeral, when the vast crowds saw a star fall from heaven as his coffin was lowered into the ground – all this contributed to the legend which began to take shape before his body was cold in the grave. Yet, though it was a legend which fed avidly on the details of his life and death, it was not confined to those details, but touched something that lay even deeper in Irish consciousness. As the career of Daniel O'Connell had already shown, the needs of a repressed but emerging nationalism had led the people in time past to invest their leader with the power and status of a Messiah who would redeem them out of their captivity. If this was true of O'Connell, it was even truer of Parnell who, aloof and majestic, embodied, to a degree no one had previously approached, the idea of the prophetic figure destined to lead Israel to the promised land. Even Gladstone, though not intending to be complimentary, had seized upon the Mosaic analogy as early as 1881. On the eve of imprisoning Parnell in Kilmainham Jail because of his Land League activities, he had described him as desiring to frustrate the working of the new Land Act, 'to stand as Moses stood between the living and the dead; to stand there, not as Moses stood, to arrest but to extend the plague.'[1]

The comparison with Moses was used again during the agony of the split by Parnell himself. 'If I am to leave you', he said at a moment when compromise seemed near, '. . . I should like – and it is not an unfair thing for me to ask – that I should come within sight of the promised land.'[2] And ten months later, on the day Parnell died, Yeats took up the same theme in that banal poem, 'Mourn – and then Onward', which he had the good sense never to reprint. He ended his embarrassing verses with these lines:

> Mourn – and then onward, there is no returning,
> He guides ye from the tomb;
> His memory now is a tall pillar, burning
> Before us in the gloom.[3]

But it was not only the *memory* of Parnell that glimmered through the political darkness that followed his death. The shock of finality was so great that some could not face it, could not concede that the Chief really had left them for ever. When he died his temperature had been so high that his body had had to be encased in a lead coffin, before being put into an oak casket. This then became so heavy that the story at once went round that it had been filled with stones, or with someone else's weightier body, that he was not dead at all, and would return to the leadership.[4] The Parnellite newspaper which published Yeats's effusion, printed others within a few days of Parnell's death which showed clearly enough how hard it was to come to terms with reality. In one of these Katharine Tynan spoke of, and in a sense for, Ireland:

> Tonight and many a night in restless slumber
>   She'll dream you are not dead
> And wake to weep sick tears without number
>   O'er your beloved head.[5]

Within a few years of this, Lady Gregory heard an old man in

71

county Galway haranguing a crowd in Irish and was told that he was saying over and over again 'he is living, he is living.'[6] She herself then went on to write *The Deliverer*, which was not only a Moses play about Parnell, but ended on a note of doubt as to whether he was actually dead or not. And so persistent was this aspect of the myth that as late as 1917 Lennox Robinson could build his play, *The Lost Leader*, on the assumption (in fact, historically wrong) that no one had ever seen Parnell in his coffin and that he therefore might have lived on into the era of the 1916 Rising.

Yet the Mosaic analogy, and the hankering after a second coming, were not the most fundamental legacies of the Parnell split. Far more important, and psychologically far more devastating, was the realisation that the fall of Parnell was essentially the work of his fellow-countrymen. Traditionally, it had been too easy for Irishmen to blame their misfortunes upon the foreign oppressor, but although in 1890–91 English pressure – from the Nonconformist churches and from the Liberal party – was certainly an important element in the final disaster, there was no denying the inescapable fact that what determined Parnell's fate was that a majority of his party voted for his deposition, and that they were subsequently upheld at the polls by an even greater majority of the voters at large. To the minority who remained loyal to him beyond the grave, his rejection was an act of betrayal which poisoned the political life of the country for a generation. Parnell himself had used the term 'betrayal' many times in the last months of his life, and at the very beginning of the crisis, in his manifesto to the Irish people which preceded the debate in Committee Room Fifteen, had demanded that he be not thrown 'to the English wolves now howling for my destruction.'

That phrase, and the act of repudiation it signified, were seized upon by the myth-makers with rare unanimity. We know from the mere title of Joyce's poem of 1891, 'Et Tu, Healy', that the analogy of Caesar stabbed by Brutus was present to his infant mind, but later, in *A Portrait of the Artist as a Young Man*, the ferocity of the Christmas dinner scene revolves round the betrayal of Parnell, the 'dead king', by 'the priests and the priests' pawns.' And the book closes on the same note. When Stephen is preparing for exile, determined to 'fly by' the nets of nationality, language and religion, he repels his friend Davin with a specific reference to the split. 'No honourable and sincere man . . . has given up to you his life and his youth and his affections from the days of Tone to those of Parnell but you sold him to the enemy or failed him in need or reviled him and left him for another.'[7]

This motif recurs in the articles Joyce wrote for Italian newspapers in the early years of his exile. Thus in 1907, a piece about Home Rule allowed him to castigate the Irish parliamentary party as a set of self-seeking hypocrites. 'They have given proof of their altruism only in 1891, when they sold their leader, Parnell, to the pharisaical conscience of the English Dissenters without exacting the thirty pieces of silver.'[8] And five years later he brought the Judas theme and the throwing to the wolves together in a few scalding sentences in 'L'Ombra di Parnell':

> The melancholy which invaded his mind was perhaps the profound conviction that, in his hour of need, one of the disciples who dipped his hand in the same bowl with him would betray him. . . . In his final desperate appeal to his fellow-countrymen he begged them not to throw him as a sop to the English wolves howling around them. It redounds to their honour that they did not fail this appeal. They did not throw him to the English wolves; they tore him to pieces themselves.[9]

Joyce, admittedly, was a special case – a bad case, as I have described him elsewhere, of arrested Parnellism.[10] This was in part hereditary, but in part due also to his own inner necessity to identify himself and his chosen lonely road with Christ or Caesar, symbolised by the local and easily realisable figure of Parnell. But others, who were under no such compulsion, were drawn inexorably towards the same, or similar, images of betrayal as being central to the myth. Lady Gregory, for instance, even improved upon history by having her Moses/Parnell in *The Deliverer* thrown not to the wolves, but to the cats. Thirty years after Parnell's death Yeats could still recall a phrase of Goethe's much quoted at the time: 'The Irish seem to me like a pack of hounds, always dragging down some noble stag.'[11] And in old age, returning once more to the same theme, it was

The Bishops and the Party
That tragic story made,

F. S. L. Lyons

A husband that had sold his wife,
And after that betrayed.[12]

The *idée fixe* of betrayal runs through so much of the literature
that grew out of the Parnell split that it would be easy to exaggerate
the preoccupation of contemporaries with it. Yet, in reality, what is
most remarkable about the Parnell literature is that it does not
begin to be significant until the early years of the twentieth century.
For this curious hiatus there are two possible explanations. The
obvious political explanation is that the division between Parnell's
followers and his opponents not only continued for nine years after
his death, but reached new depths of bitterness and ignominy. While
this struggle raged it was difficult to obtain a hearing for the exalted
view of Parnell inherent in the myth, the more so since anti-
Parnellism claimed the vast majority of votes, was deeply en-
trenched in the press, and probably represented with a fair degree
of accuracy the mood of the time.

The second explanation links the political situation with the
cultural situation. The most immediate effect of the long quarrel
between Parnellites and anti-Parnellites was that young men of
intelligence and enthusiasm became increasingly alienated by the
parliamentary party and turned in different directions. Some turned
towards the Gaelic League, founded two years after Parnell's death.
Others turned back towards the physical force movement with
results that were to be powerfully apparent in the next generation.
Yet others turned towards the new gospel of Sinn Féin, emphasising
the need for self-sufficiency at every level of the national being.

There is enough evidence here of vigorous and variegated life
to justify in broad terms the famous diagnosis which Yeats made
in the lecture he delivered in Stockholm on receiving the Nobel
Prize. 'The modern literature of Ireland', he asserted, 'and indeed
all that stir of thought which prepared for the Anglo-Irish war,
began when Parnell fell from power in 1891. A disillusioned and
embittered Ireland turned from parliamentary politics; an event
was conceived; and the race began, as I think, to be troubled by
that event's long gestation.'[13]

Like many of Yeats's more high-flown generalisations, this con-
trives to combine factual inaccuracy with psychological insight. In
reality, the way had been prepared for a cultural revival long before
the death of Parnell. The emphasis upon Irish literature, history

74

and language which seemed so urgent in the 1890s had already been anticipated by Young Ireland, and the work of Young Ireland could not have been built upon had not the antiquarians and the scholars unearthed the texts which laid the basis for the literature. And more immediately, that seminal book, Standish O'Grady's bardic *History of Ireland*, had appeared between 1878 and 1880, *before* Parnell had risen to his full authority. Also, if at an earthier level, the Gaelic Athletic Association, the first practical manifestation of the new spirit, had been founded as far back as 1884. Even Yeats himself had produced his *Poems and Ballads of Young Ireland* in 1888, while Parnell was still riding high.

Yet there was a sense in which Yeats was right to emphasise that the political paralysis which followed Parnell's death offered a supreme opportunity for a cultural movement to take root and burgeon. With that movement we are not here directly concerned. What does concern us, however, is that its development by no means followed the course mapped out for it by Yeats. Almost at once he began to quarrel with those who set propaganda above art, and the early history of the new theatre that was so essential a part of the movement, soon became a history of conflict to establish and maintain the freedom of the artist in face of the various forms of 'obscurantism' Yeats found around him.[14]

The conflict, though at times exhilarating, was also bruising, and it involved for Yeats and his fellow-workers much disenchantment with the narrow and rabid nationalism of some sections of the Irish-Ireland school, a nationalism which seemed to regard every criticism as a betrayal. The story is familiar enough and to pursue it would seem to take us far away from Parnell. Yet this is not wholly so. Because, the more the writers of the new movement collided with the bigotry of their opponents, the more they came to believe that their battle was essentially the same battle Parnell had fought and lost in 1891.

I shall try to suggest later that this, though partly true, was a dangerous over-simplification, but to understand why it was possible for so many creative minds to make such an assumption, we have first to realise that just at this time Parnellite biography was underpinning Parnellite myth. In 1898 there appeared a book which no student of Parnell has ever since been able to ignore. This was the two volume *Life* by R. Barry O'Brien. O'Brien was himself a Parnellite who was particularly close to his leader during the final

crisis. His book is not uncritical and it drew attention to some of
Parnell's peculiarities in a not always flattering way – for example,
his superstition, his unpunctuality, his laziness, his lack of literary
culture, his inarticulateness, his indifference to other people's feelings and opinions. From the historian's point of view the book is
often inadequate, both in its information and in its interpretation
of Parnell's career. All the same, the biographer got close enough
to his subject to give a picture of the man which was recognisably
true, even if it was not the whole truth. He was especially successful in conveying a whole range of characteristics which contributed
powerfully to the stereotype which from this time onward formed
the basis of the myth – Parnell's gift of silence, his strength of will,
his tenacity, his hatred of England, his ability to straddle the gap
between constitutional and violent politics, his pride, his self-
control, above all the extraordinary effect he could achieve of combining ice and fire at the same moment.

From all of this it was possible to derive a view of Parnell which
saw him as aloof, aristocratic, enigmatic, disdainful, the self-
contained and self-confident man of action riding magnificently
over the fears and hesitations of base humanity. This was a large
burden for any myth to carry – too large, and too perilous, as it
turned out – but to men and women of imagination who were
struggling to maintain their own high view of the autonomy of
literature and art, Parnell, the aristocrat who could confront the
mob and subdue it, was a powerfully seductive symbol.

We have seen already that from the day of his death this symbol
of Parnell as hero had fed the Messianic impulses to which nearly
all the leaders of the literary renaissance were sensitive. At the
opening of the new century the symbol began to take a central place
in their work. The first to use it for dramatic, as distinct from
polemical, purposes was, improbable though it may seem, George
Moore, when in 1900 he laid violent hands upon Edward Martyn's
inoffensive play, *The Tale of a Town*, and turned it into *The Bending of the Bough*. The play concerns a struggle for survival by the
impoverished town of Northhaven (signifying Ireland), which is
oppressed by its wealthy neighbour Southhaven (England). The
inhabitants of Northhaven believe they have found their Messiah
in Jasper Dean, a man of action who, despite his Southhaven ante-
cedents, or rather because of them, imposes his leadership upon
the townspeople. 'It is for that very reason', another character says

to him, 'your appeal is stronger because you are not of the people; you are the romantic element outside them, the delight they follow always.'[15] In the end, however, Dean, in obvious parallel with Parnell, sacrifices public duty for private bliss with the woman he loves. Northaven thereupon subsides into disorder to await a new redeemer.

The evidence that Moore initially cast himself in a similar Messianic role is scattered through the pages of *Hail and Farewell*. His very return home, we are to understand, savoured of the miraculous. Sickened, he insists, by the materialism of an England immersed in the Boer War, intrigued by what he already knew from Yeats and Edward Martyn of the new creative ferment at work in Ireland, he finally yielded to the lure when he heard a voice within him saying, not once but thrice, 'Go to Ireland'.[16] The hilarious adventures that befell him there form the staple of *Hail and Farewell* and, though that book's connection with the Parnell myth might seem tenuous at first sight, the myth is absolutely essential to Moore's purpose. The key is to be found in his apparently excessive emphasis on Wagner and especially in the famous pilgrimage to Bayreuth which afforded so much good clean fun at Edward Martyn's expense. Bayreuth, of course, was a Holy Place whose Messiah had been Wagner. And, as *Hail and Farewell* unfolds, it becomes clear that Moore intends a parallel between himself and Siegfried, a parallel based on the idea that Parnell's (Sigmund's) mantle had fallen upon him. First, however, he has to make it clear that Parnell's mantle had not fallen on Edward Martyn, who was under the unfortunate impression that it had. 'He was to me a pathetic figure as he sat sunning himself in the light of Ibsen and Parnell, his exterior placid as a parish priest's. . . . He is thinking that his dreams are coming to pass, and believes himself to be the Messiah – he who will give Ireland literature and her political freedom; and I wondered how far he would go before puncturing like all the others.'[17]

Yet, if poor Martyn was cast as no more than a pinchbeck Parsifal, it is significant that Moore fully reveals his own far more glittering role only at the very end of the book, when out of the depths of his disillusionment he is on the eve of leaving Ireland for the last time. During his pilgrimage he has learned that repudiation is an essential part of the Messianic condition and he is content to act out the part of one ignored and despised by his fellow-countrymen. Being Moore, however, he insists on leaving them his sacred book, his *Hail and Farewell*. Wandering out into the garden opposite his house in Ely Place, he defines the faith that had inspired his mission of redemption in a passage which, though often quoted, must be repeated here because it is so central to my theme:

> I have come into the most impersonal country in the world to preach personality . . . and I walked across the greensward afraid to leave the garden, and to heighten my inspiration I looked towards the old apple-tree, remembering that many had striven to draw forth the sword that Wotan had struck into the tree about which Hunding had built his hut. Parnell, like Sigmund, had drawn it forth, but Wotan had allowed Hunding to strike him with his spear. And the allegory becoming clearer I asked myself if I were Siegfried, son of Sigmund slain by Hunding, and if it were my fate to reforge the sword. . . .[18]

This high, romantic view of Parnell not only allowed the writers to use him as a Messianic symbol, but more important – because more immediately comprehensible to those around them – it allowed them also to use him as an ideal against which the meanness and inadequacy of the society that rejected him and them could be measured. Both Joyce and Yeats, so divergent in almost all else, were at least at one in this, that Parnell served them superbly as a weapon in their war against the alien forces with which they felt themselves to be contending. It is true that their definitions of alien forces were by no mean identical – Joyce, after all, at one time thought that Yeats had sold out to 'the trolls' and become an alien force himself – but they had enough in common to want to project Parnell as an image of nobility overcome by baseness for the purpose of castigating the baseness of their own day.[19]

Their methods could hardly have been more different. To a large extent, no doubt, this was because their conceptions of the role of the artist were at opposite poles. But this difference sprang also, I think, from the fact that whereas for Yeats Parnell was essentially a literary property like Cuchulainn – sometimes, indeed, indistinguishable from him – Joyce was closer to the ground and more directly involved. He had grown up inside the Parnellite tradition and he knew, far more intimately than Yeats could ever know, the

78

pettiness, the frustration, the sheer human fallibility, of nationalist politics at the grass roots. Thus, although Parnell offered both men a model on which to base their own public behaviour, only Joyce had access to patterns of thought and speech which enabled him to use the dead chief, or his memory, as a means of illustrating the Dublin paralysis.

It was in 'Ivy Day in the Committee Room', the story in *Dubliners* which he himself liked best, that Joyce came nearest to matching the 'scrupulous meanness' of his style to the realities of the situation he was describing. Indeed, if we compare Mr Hynes's poem on the death of Parnell with Mr Yeats's poem 'Mourn – and then Onward', we may have an uneasy sensation of art outstripping life. For Yeats's piece, though composed with a sharp eye to immediate saleability, arrived at its bathos through a kind of sincerity, springing from the emotion of the moment. Joyce, however, contrived to go beyond Yeats's genuine banality by deliberately creating an even worse poem which not only embodies in itself the post-Parnellite futility, but also attracts precisely the compliment – 'Mr Crofton said that it was a very fine piece of writing' – that damns irrevocably both the piece and the audience.

He is dead. Our Uncrowned King is dead.
O, Erin, mourn with grief and woe
For he lies dead whom the fell gang
Of modern hypocrites laid low.[20]

This, as Frank O'Connor once remarked of the whole story, is 'the mock heroic at its poker-faced deadliest.'[21]

What I am really saying, I suppose, is that although Joyce was certainly sympathetic to the Parnellite myth, it was the Parnellite actuality which provided as it were the ground bass of his work. For complex reasons – of art, of personality, of background – this way could not be Yeats's way. So that when he too encountered the Dublin paralysis, it was the myth not the actuality that he evoked. Through all the controversies which surrounded the theatre in the early years of the new century, he fortified himself by reference to Parnell's solitary splendour. 'Moses', he wrote, 'was little good to his people until he had killed an Egyptian; and for the most part a writer or public man of the upper classes is useless to this country until he has done something which separates him from his class.'[22]

The theatre certainly achieved this for Yeats – perhaps more accurately, it intensified an alienation of which John O'Leary and Maud Gonne had much earlier sown the seeds. But it was not a question merely of alienation. It was a question of right conduct, of an appropriate life-style. In ordering his conduct, in shaping that style, Yeats seized eagerly upon what he took to be a leading characteristic of Parnell's and used it as his own mask. That characteristic was Parnell's ability to keep great passion in subjection and thus to present to the world an impassive, rock-like front. This, Yeats excitedly told his actors, was what they must do also when speaking verse. 'The passion of the verse comes from the fact that the speakers are holding down violence or madness. . . . All depends on the completeness of the holding down, on the stirring of the beast underneath.'[23]

And this was how he comported himself when he had to confront the anger of the mob – whether on behalf of Synge or later on behalf of O'Casey – quelling opposition by force of personality, even, on one occasion, reducing a crowd to silence by reciting majestically the name 'Charles . . . Stewart . . . Parnell' and then delivering a speech that had nothing to do with those magic syllables. As he himself put it: 'If one remembers the men who have dominated Ireland for the last 150 years, one understands that it is strength of personality, the individualising quality in a man, that stirs Irish imagination most deeply in the end. There is scarcely a man who has led the Irish people, at any time, who may not give some day to a great writer precisely the symbol he may require for the expression of himself.'[24]

Yet Parnell's re-entry into Yeats's writing came about less through his own direct experience of Irish philistinism than from his anger at the treatment meted out to Lady Gregory's nephew, Sir Hugh Lane, when his imaginative project to endow Dublin with a gallery of modern art failed for various reasons – not least because wealthy men – Lord Ardilaun and W. M. Murphy – declined to make substantial contributions where there was no proven need for such a gallery. That Murphy should have taken this line was for Yeats a particular aggravation, not merely because Murphy's paper, the *Irish Independent*, moulded and expressed the bourgeois Catholic attitudes he had earlier confronted over the plays of Synge, but because Murphy, along with T. M. Healy and his relatives ('the Sullivan gang' as Yeats called them) had taken an active part in the deposition of Parnell.[25] All these things came together in the bitter ironies of 'To a Shade'.

> A man
> Of your own passionate serving kind who had brought
> In his full hands what, had they only known,
> Had given their children's children loftier thought,
> Sweeter emotion, working in their veins
> Like gentle blood, has been driven from the place,
> And insult heaped upon him for his pains,
> And for his open-handedness, disgrace;
> Your enemy, an old foul mouth, had set
> The pack upon him.[26]

The date written below the poem is 29 September 1913. Earlier that month a former Parnellite, William O'Brien, had published some reminiscent articles in which he claimed that when the true facts about the O'Shea affair were known, 'the Irish leader would have been shown to be rather a victim than a destroyer of a happy home.' Captain O'Shea was by then dead, but his son Gerard, zealous for his father's reputation, persuaded his mother to publish her own memoirs which appeared in the spring of 1914 as *Charles Stewart Parnell: his Love Story and Political Life*. With the publication of this extraordinary book, the first cracks in the heroic myth began to develop. Intended primarily to buttress the story told by Captain O'Shea in the divorce-court – that he had been a deceived husband for no less than nine years – Katharine's memoirs revealed two aspects of Parnell which were severely damaging to the traditional image of him. One was that already by 1881 he was so besotted with his amour that he was prepared, in certain circumstances, to abandon public life altogether. And the other, perhaps even more deadly to his posthumous career as a literary myth, was that his epistolary style belonged rather to the school of Mr Pooter than to that of Don Juan. The endearments he lavished upon Mrs O'Shea – she was his 'Queen', his 'darling Queenie', his 'own little Wifie' – were never, of course, intended to be made public and no one would have been more acutely embarrassed than Parnell himself if this had happened in his lifetime.

When it happened in 1914 it produced mixed results. Yeats, for example, drew from the book only further evidence of the Parnell he wanted to believe in – the man of passion beneath the man of ice. What impressed him most was the story Katharine told of Parnell holding her over a boiling sea at the end of a Brighton pier, ready to jump with her into oblivion if she gave the slightest sign of fear. That Yeats was deeply stirred by this we know from the fact that he referred to it twice – in *A Vision* and in *The Trembling of the Veil*. In the latter he tells us why. 'What excitement there would have been, what sense of mystery would have stirred all our hearts . . . had we known the story Mrs Parnell tells of that scene on Brighton pier. . . . Perhaps unmotived self-immolation, were that possible, or else at mere suggestion of storm and night, were as great evidence as such a man could give of power over self, and so of the expression of self.'[27]

This was one way of looking at Katharine's book. But there was another way and, predictably, it was Joyce, sensitive as always to the squalid realities of the split, who expressed most clearly the shock of disenchantment her narrative caused among the faithful. It was not merely that her habit of calling Parnell 'King' must have caused the author of the Christmas Dinner scene – where Mr Casey laments 'my dead king' – to wince rather sharply. It was much more that the entire love-affair seemed to have an alien air about it. In his preparatory notes for the play *Exiles* he observed that Katharine's book had not helped him to explore the psychology of woman (though her Spanish experiences may have given him some hints towards Molly Bloom), 'firstly because Parnell was tongue-tied and secondly because she was an Englishwoman. Her manner of writing is not Irish – nay, her manner of loving is not Irish. The character of O'Shea is much more typical of Ireland.'[28] In this last remark, as Herbert Howarth has pointed out, there may lurk a hidden significance – that Joyce, who in 1909 had suffered the anguish of believing (falsely) that he had been cuckolded by his friend Cosgrave and thereafter developed a sympathy for husbands in that condition, may have found in O'Shea an early intimation of Bloom.[29] Joyce being Joyce, however, this did not prevent him from endowing Bloom with certain characteristics that were indubitably Parnellite – a love of flowers, a predilection for scientific experiment, and an interest in Sir Robert Ball's work on astronomy.

But in his anxious scanning of Katharine's memoirs Joyce, as so often, was in a minority of one. Despite some outcries in the press, the book fell flat. Partly, no doubt, this was because of the onset of the war. Partly, and more directly, it was because the Home Rule crisis had once again quickened the pace of Irish politics and suddenly precipitated a new phase of the old debate between the moderates and the men of violence. In this resurrected debate the Parnell myth continued to serve as a point of reference for different traditions of political nationalism which had little else in common. His official heirs were the parliamentary party who until 1918 were led by John Redmond, upon whom in 1891 the dead Chief's mantle had fallen. But Arthur Griffith, the founder of Sinn Féin, had also been a Parnellite in his youth and as late as 1917 still proclaimed his loyalty to his old leader, who had anticipated, even if he had failed to implement, the Sinn Féin policies of economic self-sufficiency and of withdrawal from the British parliament.[30]

But neither Griffith nor Connolly nor Pearse allowed sufficiently for Parnell's political opportunism, his almost cynical realism, his ability to cloak his inmost thoughts in deliberate ambiguity. Each wanted to annexe him, who fitted into no single category, as a progenitor of his own highly individual point of view. Connolly, for example, seized on one undoubted fact about Parnell's last struggle – that he appealed to the working-class for support. Contemporaries correctly diagnosed this as a clear case of a drowning man clutching at any kind of life-belt. But within seven years of Parnell's death we find Connolly using the episode to demonstrate the irrelevance of Parnellites and anti-Parnellites alike to the cause of the proletariat:

> During the early days of the split Mr Parnell did, indeed, adopt a programme laid before him by Dublin workingmen, . . . but with his untimely death disappeared every hope of seeing that programme adhered to by any Home Rule party. Every succeeding year has seen the Parnellite party becoming more and more conservative and reactionary. . . .
> Followers of Parnell they are indeed, but they follow at such a respectable distance they have lost sight not only of the leader but of his principles.[31]

If Connolly could see in Parnell a forerunner, however improbable, of the workers' republic, Pearse was quite sure that he belonged to the older tradition of the republic *pur sang*. In the famous pamphlet of 1915, for which he borrowed from Ibsen the title 'Ghosts', Pearse enumerated the founding fathers of Irish nationality, the men who had thought the problem through and spread the gospel to their contemporaries. Having listed four of these, Wolfe Tone, Thomas Davis, James Fintan Lalor and John Mitchel, he continued:

> If one had to add a fifth to the four I have named, the fifth would inevitably be Parnell. Now, Parnell was less a political thinker than an embodied conviction; a flame that seared, a sword that stabbed. He deliberately disclaimed political theories, deliberately confined himself to political action. . . . His instinct was a separatist instinct; and far from being prepared to accept Home Rule as 'a final settlement between the two nations', he was always careful to make it clear that whether Home Rule came or did not come, the way must be left open for the achievement of the greater thing.[32]

In all of this there was some truth, though it was not the whole truth. But there was, of course, a sense in which Pearse himself belonged to the Parnellite myth, because he too was imbued with the Messianic idea, which lay at the root of his play, *The Singer*. There, the hero, MacDara, clearly states the ultimate sacrifice which the role demands. 'One man can free a people as one man redeemed the world. I will take no pike. I will go into battle with bare hands. I will stand up before the Gall as Christ hung naked before men on a tree.'[33] 'When Pearse summoned Cuchulainn to his side, what stalked through the Post Office?', Yeats asked in after years. One answer might well be – Parnell.

And yet all that delirium of the brave did not last. Easter 1916 led to the transformation of Sinn Féin. The triumph of Sinn Féin in the general election of 1918 led to the Anglo-Irish War. The Anglo-Irish War led to the Treaty of 1921 which set the seal upon a partitioned Ireland. This in turn led to the Civil War and the hatred which distorted the generation that grew up in the shadow of that catastrophe. After the frenzy of any revolution, disenchantment is the common reaction. But when the frenzy ends as it did in Ireland, the disenchantment is apt to be deep and crippling. And so began the long recoil of literature from a reality that fell far short of the dream that had sustained writers and men of action alike in the years between the death of Parnell and the death of Pearse.

The pre-eminent spokesman for this phase of recoil was Yeats, the Yeats who, having made his gesture of reconciliation by returning to live permanently in Ireland in 1922, slipped quickly again into his familiar role of critic and castigator of a society which at once fascinated and repelled him. It is clear from his letters, and from the speeches he began to make after his election to the Senate in 1922, that within a very few years he had come to believe that not only his artistic beliefs, but the whole Anglo-Irish tradition from which he sprang, were menaced by the same forces – ignorance, bigotry, 'the obscure spite of our old Paudeen in his shop' – that he had fought in the early years of the century. Only now those forces were, so to speak, institutionalised. They represented power, wealth, respectability, and they had created a nation which contrived to be both 'belated' (Joyce's word) and complacent.

Against this Catholic bourgeois nationalism Yeats once more took up the cudgels. I am not concerned here with the details of his struggle, with the diagnosis of his conservatism, or with exploring the strange paths along which that conservatism took him. But what is relevant to my theme is the re-entry of Parnell into his work in the mid-1930s, just at the very moment when he had abandoned any fleeting hope he might have cherished that the Blueshirt movement would lead to that 'despotism of the educated classes' he continually craved for at this time.[34] 'Parnell's Funeral' is of crucial importance here, for it brings together with a controlled ferocity ideas and memories that had been part of his intellectual life for many years – the contempt for O'Connell, 'the Great Comedian'; the recollection of the star that had fallen from the sky at Parnell's funeral; his own famous vision in 1896 of the woman shooting an arrow at a star; the concept of sacrifice and rebirth when the heart of the sacrificed hero is eaten; the old preoccupation with *hysterica passio*, though not this time as passion kept in check by the strong will of the great man, rather as passion unchecked and so dragging the quarry down; the recurrent theme of betrayal, and especially betrayal as an Irish phenomenon.

None shared our guilt; nor did we play a part
Upon a painted stage when we devoured his heart.

The devastating political impact of the poem comes precisely
from its repudiation of the assumption – so deeply held for so long
– that, the heart of the hero once devoured, it will beat again in
the coming Messiah.

Come, fix upon me that accusing eye.
I thirst for accusation. All that was sung,
All that was said in Ireland was a lie
Bred out of the contagion of the throng,
Saving the song rats hear before they die.

Even so, he cannot let the legend be. There would have been a
rebirth, a regeneration, if Parnell's heart had been eaten; but the
legend was not lived out to its final act:

Had de Valera eaten Parnell's heart
No loose-lipped demagogue had won the day,
No civil rancour torn the land apart.

Had Cosgrave eaten Parnell's heart, the land's
Imagination had been satisfied,
Or lacking that, government in such hands,
O'Higgins its sole statesman had not died.

Had even O'Duffy – but I name no more – [35]

So Parnell, equated at the end with Swift, plucks 'bitter wisdom
that enriched his blood.' And for those who are left, there remains
only the bleak indifference of the couplet written a little later:

Parnell came down the road, he said to a cheering man:
'Ireland shall get her freedom and you still break stone.'[36]

Yet this was not quite the end. In 1931, Henry Harrison, who as
a young man had fought at Parnell's side in his last struggle and
had afterwards helped Katharine through the early stages of her
widowhood, published his *Parnell Vindicated*. This was based on

conversations he had with her soon after Parnell's death and it threw new light on the Parnell–O'Shea triangle. According to Katharine, her husband (as many people had long suspected) had known of her affair with Parnell almost from the beginning and had stayed silent for nearly nine years, partly because he had political ambitions which he hoped – at least until 1886 – that Parnell could satisfy, and partly because he expected to share in the large fortune Katharine was to inherit from her rich 'Aunt Ben', Mrs Wood, who was already 88 years old when the liaison began. This aunt had maintained Katharine and her husband in separate establishments for many years, but although she did indeed leave her estate to her niece when she died in 1889, the will was contested by other members of the family. For this reason, Katharine was unable to raise the £20,000 in return for which, she alleged, Captain O'Shea was prepared to allow her to divorce him. The expectation that this would be the sequence of events had enabled Parnell to assure some of his friends before the divorce came on, that he would emerge without stain from the ordeal. But when the money was not forthcoming, the Captain, who may have had political as well as personal reasons for wishing to destroy Parnell, launched his thunderbolt, with results that are part of history. Parnell was anxious above all to secure a divorce and so was not represented in court. But for this he had to pay a heavy price, since the worst possible construction could, without fear of contradiction, be placed upon the various devices to ensure secrecy which he and Katharine had employed for almost a decade; devices ironically enough, which were as necessary to O'Shea as to themselves. The contrast between Parnell's pre-divorce assurances and the sorry tale of aliases and rented houses that was unfolded in the divorce-court, probably did more than anything else to blast his reputation amongst the guardians of conventional morality in England and Ireland.[37]

Five years after publishing *Parnell Vindicated*, Harrison offered Yeats a copy of the book. The author was then over sixty, but his letter still breathed the hero-worship of his youth. 'Parnell's part in these things', he wrote, 'never ceases to fill me with amazement even though I knew him and appraised him as a demi-god – such vision, such simplicity, such concentrated passion.'[38] This letter led to a meeting between the two men. The poet found the politician 'a man broken by time' (in fact, Harrison lived to be nearly ninety), but in a record he made of the visit Yeats fastened at once upon the essence of the story, and soon afterwards wrote the verses, 'Come gather round me, Parnellites'. 'I thought', he noted, 'that they might suggest to somebody that there was nothing discreditable in Parnell's love for his mistress and his wife.'[39] This ballad, with its jaunty rhythms, is a far cry from 'To a Shade' or 'Parnell's Funeral', yet it contains one final recognition of that pre-eminent quality which had throughout his life attracted the writer to the man of action:

> For Parnell was a proud man,
> No prouder trod the ground,
> And a proud man's a lovely man,
> So pass the bottle round.[40]

'So pass the bottle round.' It might almost be an epitaph. Parnell, indeed, continued into the 1960s to cast a shadow over Irish writing, but less as a Messianic symbol than as a touchstone for various kinds of disenchantment. This was true, though in different ways, of O'Faoláin, O'Connor and O'Casey. Disenchantment is at its bleakest perhaps in O'Faoláin's *Bird Alone*, where Parnell is equated with the colour and excitement that went out of Irish life when the Chief died. The anti-hero of that novel, returning from London and looking stonily at the spiritual desert around him, sums it up in a single devastating sentence. 'But then as I stood there, I realised suddenly that in those dead years in which I lived, the years after Parnell, the shore of Ireland was empty too, and would remain empty for a long time, and that I was merely one of many left stranded by the storm.'[41] Frank O'Connor, admittedly, was much less afflicted by this paralysing nostalgia, but even he, confronting the, for him, still more terrible tragedy of Michael Collins, sought refuge in a Parnellite parallel. 'His work done, the Ireland he loved set free, he himself would personify a mass-possession even greater than that Parnell had stood for, and from his body, struck down in its glory, the intellect of the nation would once more pass into the wilderness.'[42]

Sean O'Casey's disenchantment had quite other roots, but it led him to a strikingly similar conclusion. He sharply recalls us to something that historians and critics are equally prone to forget – the irrelevance of the public drama of politics to the poor whose struggle for survival occupies them to the exclusion of all else.

The first volume of his *Autobiographies* makes this point brilliantly, in the contrast between the misery of his mother, carrying home the body of one of her dead children, when her cab is trapped by the Parnell funeral, and the facile ecstasy of the cab-driver who apostrophises 'Ireland's greatest son' in a manner worthy of Joyce's meanness at its most scrupulous.[43] Yet O'Casey himself cannot wholly resist the Messianic analogy, when his turn comes to leave the city of his triumph and rejection. Taking his melancholy way through the Dublin streets he comes at last to Westland Row Station, his point of departure, Parnell's point of arrival. 'It was from this sad site that the coffin holding Parnell came slowly out, borne by strenuous, tearful men, hesitating to part even with the dead body of their persecuted chieftain.'[44]

This was not the end of the literary reverberation of Parnell, but it marks a dying fall. Plays continued to be written, either about him or under his influence (Frank O'Connor and Padraic Colum were the two most eminent exponents, but there were at least four others), and even as recently as 1963 Michael Farrell's novel, *Thy Tears Might Cease*, offered a late example of the artist-rebel taking heart from the solitary pride of the long-dead leader. Yet, two qualifying remarks have to be made about these modern manifestations of the myth. The first is that in none of them does Parnell play a central or dynamic role. And the second is that there has been an increasing tendency to write about him as a real person, even to the extent of embodying actual dialogue from the debate in Committee Room Fifteen or other contemporary sources. The myth, in short, has been invaded by history, and it is time to ask in conclusion how far history diverges from the myth.

In the strict sense the reconstruction of the historical Parnell begins only with the publication of Dr Conor Cruise O'Brien's *Parnell and his Party* in 1957. There had indeed been biographical studies by St John Ervine in 1925 and by Joan Haslip in 1937, but Irvine's book was distorted by bias, and Miss Haslip's, though not without insight, was superficial and under-researched. Dr Cruise O'Brien achieved a brilliant *tour de force* by directing attention away from the love-affair and towards Parnell as a practising politician. In no sense a biography, his book was an admirable analysis of the parliamentary party Parnell created, of how he governed it, and of the impact it made upon Anglo-Irish relations. The Parnell that emerged had indeed some of the characteristics of the mythical Parnell – his pride, his aloofness, his dictatorial tendencies – but he had also his share of human frailty. He was a man who could make mistakes, lose his temper, alienate his friends, indulge in ambiguities and inconsistencies seemingly without end.

Nevertheless, for Dr Cruise O'Brien the inconsistencies are only apparent and the ambiguities are deliberately contrived to achieve specific purposes. His Parnell is at bottom a conservative who manages, until the last act, to harness both revolutionists and constitutionalists in pursuit of a severely practical and limited programme of self-government. After the traumatic experience of the Land War, he swings rapidly from the time of his imprisonment in Kilmainham towards an emphasis on House of Commons action which allows him to use the Irish vote – both there and in the constituencies – to hold the balance between the two great English parties. The crown of this achievement, in Dr Cruise O'Brien's analysis, is the conversion of Mr Gladstone to Home Rule and the alliance between the Irish and the Liberals which resulted therefrom. That alliance not only produced the epoch-making Home Rule Bill of 1886, but survived the defeat of the Bill and the partial break-up of the Liberal party, to usher in a period of Liberal-nationalist concord which, had it not been disrupted by the decisive blow of the divorce-crisis, might have led to a second and more successful bid for Home Rule when Gladstone came back to power.

With most of this analysis I concur. Where I diverge somewhat from Dr Cruise O'Brien is in my assessment of Parnell's leadership. He sees the Chief as a political genius who, most of the time, was superbly in control of his environment. I, on the contrary, believe that his control lasted for a much shorter period than is generally supposed, or was, at any rate, much more intermittent, and I am convinced that his political freedom was permanently compromised by the Liberal alliance in and after 1885. This theme was adumbrated in *The Fall of Parnell*, published in 1960, and it is carried to much greater lengths in the biography, *Charles Stewart Parnell*, which has just appeared. It would be inappropriate to develop it here in any detail, but I must refer to it briefly, because of its relevance to the question of how far the Parnell myth supports or, alternatively, distorts, historical reality.

The central fact is that although after 1886 Parnell continued to preach the doctrine of independent opposition, and from time to time to proclaim that the continued presence of his party at West-

minster was strictly provisional, in practice he was bound hand
and foot to the Liberals, since they alone could deliver Home Rule.
When, therefore, the divorce precipitated a landslide of Nonconformist protest, and when Gladstone intimated that Home Rule
could not progress while Parnell remained leader of the Irish party,
Parnell found himself forced into the position of having to ask his
party to choose between him and the policy he had brought
apparently so near success. It was not surprising and not wholly
discreditable, that they should have chosen the policy. In this they
were influenced much less by the Church than the myth would have
us believe. The bishops actually held their hands for as long as
they dared in the hope that the politicians would solve the problem without them; open and effective ecclesiastical intervention
came only after Parnell had issued his wild manifesto denouncing
the Liberal alliance and seeming to pull his own temple about his
ears. And even then, even after the party split in two, and after the
Kilkenny election, it is well to remember that Parnell could still
have marched out with the honours of war and, while resigning
the chairmanship for a period, have remained the arbiter of Home
Rule and of the fortunes of the party.

His rejection of favourable terms and the increasing vehemence
of his speeches led many contemporaries to believe that his mind
had given way and that, in his desperation, he had turned from
constitutionalism to the Fenians. Both these assumptions I believe
to be wrong. Parnell was not mad, though his pride – on his own
behalf and still more on Katharine's – had been so grievously
wounded that his fury certainly knew no bounds. This, however,
did not affect his tactical skill which, his opponents admitted, had
never been greater than in his last campaign. As for the Fenians,
though they flocked to his support and drew much comfort from
his speeches, even in the most extreme of those speeches there
were always to be found the familiar reservations. He never did
abandon the path of parliamentary politics and consistently looked
forward to the next general election as the first step towards re-
building an independent party.

The most damaging criticisms of his leadership are those which
reach much further back than the split. One might summarise them
thus. He was in general not a man of ideas, and he initiated nothing
that had not been thought of first by others. More specifically, he
had little realisation of the problems that a self-governing Ireland

would face. For example, he never succeeded in working out a satisfactory relationship with the Church; he was quite ignorant of, and certainly under-rated, Ulster Unionism, though that had already emerged as a significant force in the Home Rule crisis of 1886; he failed to define what he meant by the Irish nation he spoke of so frequently, and it seems never to have entered his head that Ireland might contain not one but two nations.

Worse than any of this, however, was the fact that for several years before the split he had virtually ceased to lead. He opposed the revival of the land agitation in and after 1886, and in his absence from the field, alternative leaders inevitably arose. Similarly, his withdrawal from the active conduct of parliamentary business meant that both the discipline and the unity of the party began to crack. In the year 1890, before the divorce trial in November, there had been a whole series of abrasive incidents which strongly suggested that Parnell would have faced grave trouble even if the leadership crisis had not developed in the way it did.

Part of Parnell's absenteeism was undoubtedly due to the near fatal illness he suffered in the winter of 1886–7. Most probably it was Bright's disease, for kidney infections continued to trouble him thereafter, and since he also suffered from acute rheumatism and a suspect heart, he remained a sick man to the end of his life. This certainly diminished his physical energies – until the reckless outpouring of the last months – and it may have affected his judgment as well.

But far more important than bad health in the general deterioration of his position, was his infatuation with Katharine O'Shea, which had already begun to distract him from his political work long before illness overtook him. Surely the most telling criticism – and the one that is ultimately most destructive of the myth – is not simply that he neglected his country for his mistress, but that he did so for ignoble motives which involved him in ignoble situations. It is indeed a measure of his enchantment that a man of his unbending pride should have submitted for so long to a course of conduct that was not only dangerous but also degrading. Yeats, in the note he made after his interview with Harrison, made this observation: 'I cannot, however, look upon Captain O'Shea as merely amusing. . . . He has endangered the future of Irish dramatic literature by making melodrama too easy, and I am a theatre director; for drama one must imagine, and I cannot imagine what

Captain O'Shea thought of himself when he looked into the mirror.'[45] It is tempting to apply the same remark to the man who supplanted Captain O'Shea.

Of course, some of the elements of the myth remained untarnished to the end. The force of Parnell's personality, his capacity for action, his ruthlessness, his obstinacy, the sheer power of his will – all these, so far from diminishing, seemed to flare up in one last conflagration before the flame wavered and sank for ever. Yet the study of his life reveals so much that is fallible and pathetic that no one can spend long in his company, however retrospectively, without becoming intensely aware that while the myth certainly said something about Parnell, it did not say all. For literature this fact may be of no particular significance. What the writers did with the myth is far more important than the materials they had to work from. But we must not forget that the myth also had a profound political impact. The model of the heroic leader sacrificed by the people was a powerfully explosive force, influencing the men of 1916 no less than the writers of the literary renaissance. And since in Ireland highly-charged political myths have a tendency to become lethal, the historian has an obligation to emphasise what Parnell was not as well as what he was. He was not, in fact, a tall pillar burning through the gloom, nor a lost leader, nor a messiah. He was a political animal of exceptional sagacity and flair who permanently influenced the history of Britain and Ireland, but who, so far from having been sacrificed by others, sacrificed his own career and his country's destiny to a passion which in the end he failed to control. Yet by his very frailty he demonstrated his humanity, so reminding us that while myths have their importance in the scheme of things, a man is a man is a man.

NOTES

1   *The Times,* 8 Oct. 1881.
2   *Freeman's Journal,* 2 Dec. 1890.
3   Allan Wade (ed.), *The Letters of W. B. Yeats* (London, 1954), p. 179; *United Ireland,* 10 Oct. 1891.
4   Henry Harrison, *Parnell Vindicated* (London, 1931), pp. 95-9.
5   *United Ireland,* 17 Oct. 1891.

6   Lady Gregory, notes on 'The Deliverer', in *Irish Folk-history Plays* (2nd series, New York and London, 1912), p. 195.

7   James Joyce, *A Portrait of the Artist as a Young Man* (*The Essential James Joyce*, London, 1948), p. 327.

8   E. Mason and R. Ellmann (ed.), *The Critical Writings of James Joyce* (London, 1959), p. 196.

9   *Ibid.*, p. 228.

10 F. S. L. Lyons, 'James Joyce's Dublin', in *Twentieth Century Studies* (Nov. 1970), p. 201.

11 W. B. Yeats, *Autobiographies* (London, 1955), p. 316.

12 W. B. Yeats, *Collected Poems* (London, 1963), p. 356.

13 W. B. Yeats, *Autobiographies*, p. 559.

14 He defined them in *United Irishman*, 24 Oct. 1903.

15 George Moore, *The Bending of the Bough* (Chicago, 1969), p. 46.

16 George Moore, *Hail and Farewell: Ave* (London, Ebury edition, 1937), pp. 282-3.

17 *Ibid.*, p. 126, John Dillon, Parnell's former lieutenant and not a man of fanciful imagination, outdid even Moore by actually seeing a vision of Parnell at Bayreuth in 1894, appropriately enough during an interval in a performance of *Götterdämmerung*. Returning through the hall, he heard a voice he immediately recognised as Parnell's:

> The words I heard him use, I had distinctly in my mind all through the opera and on my way back to the hotel. But my recollection of them has now – 12.20 – become unaccountably blurred. Unfortunately, I did not write them down on the moment. But it was a well-known phrase which I have frequently heard him use with the particular intonation wh[ich] I recognised on the instant – 'Oh, dear me, bless me, not at all.' I looked hard at him then – he was standing quite close to me . . . I did not notice the colour of his clothes, but he was carelessly dressed and had on a shooting-jacket such as I have often seen him wear, wore a brown soft felt hat. . . . His side face was turned . . . a little away, so that I could only see his whiskers and beard. It [sic] was the colour of Parnell and just as he used to wear it, jagged and untrimmed. . . .

Dillon then describes the man, though not quite so tall as Parnell, as walking with his gait. Not unnaturally shaken by this apparition, Dillon did not follow him, but continued to watch him closely:

> When he was about to turn I looked away – stupidly – and I said to myself if he disappears when he catches sight of me I shall conclude it is Parnell. I looked again in a moment and he had disappeared. . . . My action was stupid in the extreme, but the occurrence was one calculated to throw most men off their balance, and sudden action in a matter of that character has never been my 'forte' ('Diary', 27 Sept. 1894. Dillon Papers).

18 George Moore, *Hail and Farewell: Vale* (London, Ebury edition, 1937), p. 209.

19 E. Mason and R. Ellmann (ed.), *The Critical Writings of James Joyce*, pp. 71-2.

94

20 James Joyce, *Dubliners* (*The Essential James Joyce*), pp. 109-10.
21 Frank O'Connor, *The Lonely Voice: a Study of the Short Story* (London, 1963), p. 120.
22 *Samhain*, Oct. 1901.
23 Cited in H. Howarth, *The Irish Writers, 1880-1940* (London, 1958), p. 138.
24 W. B. Yeats, *Explorations* (London, 1962), pp. 147-8.
25 Allan Wade (ed.), *The Letters of W. B. Yeats*, pp. 163-4.
26 W. B. Yeats, *Collected Poems*, p. 123.
27 W. B. Yeats, *A Vision* (London, 1962 edition), p. 124, and *Autobiographies*, pp. 232-3.
28 Cited in H. Howarth, op. cit., p. 264.
29 *Ibid.*, pp. 297-9; Richard Ellmann, *The Life of James Joyce* (New York, 1959), pp. 288-93.
30 *Nationality*, 2 June 1917, S. Ó. Lúing, 'Arthur Griffith and Sinn Féin', in F. X. Martin (ed.), *Leaders and Men of the Easter Rising: Dublin, 1916* (London, 1967), p. 55.
31 *Workers' Republic*, 8 Oct. 1898.
32 P. H. Pearse, *Political Writings and Speeches* (Dublin, n.d.), pp. 241-5.
33 P. H. Pearse, *The Singer and other Plays* (Dublin, 1960), pp. 43-4.
34 Allan Wade (ed.), *The Letters of W. B. Yeats*, pp. 811-2.
35 W. B. Yeats, *Collected Poems*, pp. 319-20.
36 *Ibid.*, p. 359.
37 For these events, see F. S. L. Lyons, *The Fall of Parnell* (London, 1960), chap. 2.
38 Henry Harrison to W. B. Yeats, 23 July 1936 (letter in private possession).
39 W. B. Yeats, *Essays and Introductions* (London, 1961), p. 486.
40 W. B. Yeats, *Collected Poems*, p. 356.
41 S. O'Faoláin, *Bird Alone* (London and Dublin, paperback edition, 1973), p. 187.
42 F. O'Connor, *The Big Fellow* (paperback edition, Dublin, 1965), p. 18.
43 S. O'Casey, *Autobiographies* (2 vols., London, 1963), I, 9.
44 *Ibid.*, II, 246.
45 W. B. Yeats, *Essays and Introductions*, p. 488.

SYNGE AND THE DOORS OF PERCEPTION

ANN SADDLEMYER

This evening, after a day of teeming rain, it cleared for an hour, and I went out while the sun was setting to a little cove where a high sea was running. As I was coming back the darkness began to close in except in the west, where there was a red light under the clouds. Against this light I could see patches of open wall and little fields of stooks, and a bit of laneway with an old man driving white cows before him. These seemed transfigured beyond any description.

Then I passed two men riding bare-backed towards the west, who spoke to me in Irish, and a little further on I came to the only village on my way. The ground rose towards it, and as I came near there was a grey bar of smoke from every cottage going up to the low clouds overhead, and standing out strangely against the blackness of the mountain behind the village.

Beyond the patch of wet cottages I had another stretch of lonely roadway, and a heron kept flapping in front of me, rising and lighting again with many lonely cries that made me glad to reach the little public-house near Smerwick.[1]

In this passage which concludes his essays on West Kerry, Synge attempts to capture, with almost Wordsworthian splendour, the various sensations, images, and emotions evoked by his wanderings through the west of Ireland. The effect is deliberately cumulative: a background in time and space of sea and cove behind him, damp clouds above, sharpened by a streak of red light below from the west which frames a clearing across which move the farmer and his cattle. The panorama then shifts again with the solitary walker, skimming over a landscape empty but for two bare-backed riders who rise before him, give their soft Irish greeting, and disappear into the west; he passes a village etched against the black moun-

97

tain, joined by streaks of smoke to the lowering clouds above. His footsteps echoing along the roadway, the uncanny cry of a heron alone breaking the silence and describing great arcs through the dusk ahead, the narrator, nerves on edge, finally reaches the comforting warmth and light of 'the little public-house near Smerwick.' These could be the moments before Shawn Keogh's entrance initiates the action of *The Playboy of the Western World*; the same hushed expectancy at nightfall opens *Deirdre of the Sorrows*, *When the Moon Has Set*, and *The Shadow of the Glen*. The effect is cumulative, but each paragraph of perception is deliberately, selectively, engraved; the sharp succession of images – a man 'transfigured' against a shock of light, details of sea, landscape, and sky – are etched with nerve-end intensity.

A similar heightened consciousness of sound, sight, and smell, accompanied by a crescendo of separately spaced emotions, is evoked in the following passage from *The Aran Islands*:

> I have been down sitting on the pier till it was quite dark. I am only beginning to understand the nights of Inishmaan and the influence they have had in giving distinction to these men who do most of their work after nightfall.
>
> I could hear nothing but a few curlews and other wild-fowl whistling and shrieking in the seaweed, and the low rustling of the waves. It was one of the dark sultry nights peculiar to September, with no light anywhere except the phosphorence of the sea, and an occasional rift in the clouds that showed stars behind them.
>
> The sense of solitude was immense. I could not see or realise my own body, and I seemed to exist merely in my perception of the waves and of the crying birds, and of the smell of seaweed.
>
> When I tried to come home I lost myself among the sandhills, and the night seemed to grow unutterably cold and dejected, as I groped among slimy masses of seaweed and wet crumbling walls.
>
> After a while I heard a movement in the sand, and two grey shadows appeared beside me. They were two men who were going home from fishing. I spoke to them and knew their voices, and we went home together.[2]

Again, in this more polished work, the moment of vision is carefully rooted not only in time and place, but in the chain of sounds, sights, smells and bodily sensations leading up to, then away from, the instant of revelation. 'In Inishmaan,' Synge wrote, 'one is forced to believe in a sympathy between man and nature.'[3] But the separateness of man from nature is also emphasized, the moment of sympathy held shining for an instant of recognition, then a further shock of reaction leading to the comforting approach of fellow countrymen.

We can find examples of this heightened awareness on practically every page of *The Aran Islands*:

It has cleared, and the sun is shining with a luminous warmth that makes the whole island glisten with the splendour of a gem, and fills the sea and sky with a radiance of blue light.[4]

Similarly identified is the thrill of delight accompanying these moments of awareness. 'There is hardly an hour I am with them,' he says of the Islanders themselves, 'that I do not feel the shock of some inconceivable idea, and then again the shock of some vague emotion that is familiar to them and to me.'[5] The tremor of excitement may be as brief as poteen's 'shock of joy to the blood',[6] or it may ride out a twenty-four hour storm as he wanders amongst the curlews on the cliffs till his hair and clothing are stiff with salt:

After a few hours the mind grows bewildered with the endless change and struggle of the sea, and an utter despondency replaces the first moment of exhilaration . . .

About the sunset the clouds broke and the storm turned to a hurricane. Bars of purple cloud stretched across the sound where immense waves were rolling from the west, wreathed with snowy phantasies of spray. Then there was the bay full of green delirium, and the Twelve Pins touched with mauve and scarlet in the east.

The suggestion from this world of inarticulate power was immense, and now at midnight, when the wind is abating, I am still trembling and flushed with exaltation.[7]

It may be the frank enjoyment of danger itself, such as a wild race by curragh with the mountainous waves:

I enjoyed the passage. Down in this shallow trough of canvas, that bent and trembled with the motion of the men, I had a far more intimate feeling of the glory and power of the waves than I have ever known in a steamer.[8]

(From such a passage we gain fresh insight into Cathleen's challenge to old Maurya in *Riders to the Sea*: 'It's the life of a young man to be going on the sea . . .') Even beauty itself at such times can be dangerous, as he admits in an Aran notebook:

A heavy roll from the Atlantic is today on the north west of the island and the surf line is of wonderful splendour. I am used to it and look now backwards to the morning a few weeks ago when I looked out first unexpectedly over the higher cliffs of Aranmore, and stopped trembling with delight. A so sudden gust beautiful is a danger. It is well arranged that for the most part we do not realize the beauty of a new wonderful experience till it has grown familiar and so safe to us.[9]

Again and again it is this 'so sudden gust beautiful' that Synge attempts to catch in his writings on Ireland. And, as with Hopkins, the delight comes as much from the unexpected wonderment as from the beauty itself: 'the prized, the desirable sight, unsought, presented so easily.' Virginia Woolf would later define such a moment as 'a revelation . . . the world comes closer, swollen with some astonishing significance . . . an illumination; a match burning in a crocus; an inner meaning almost expressed.'[10] His travel essays, even the *Manchester Guardian* articles on the Congested Districts, bristle with words attempting to capture the exceptional moment: 'strange', 'curious', 'peculiar', 'wonderful', 'extraordinary', 'luminous', 'splendid', and even 'indescribable'. In nearly every case the narrator's senses are heightened, his awareness sharpened, nerves as well as blood quickened by the experience, but the incident once presented is unremarked. I have found two finished examples only, both familiar to readers of Synge and one in fact polished for republication by the author himself, that appear as 'set pieces' within the carefully crafted narrative, calling attention to themselves in an unprecedented manner. In both cases Synge by his comments deliberately draws attention to their significance, and in a special way they differ from the experiences I have already quoted.

100

The first, most familiar, comes once again from *The Aran Islands*, but was selected by Synge for prepublication in *The Green Sheaf*, a broadsheet briefly published by Pamela Colman Smith, a friend of the Yeats family; it was then reprinted with Synge's permission in the New York *Gael*.[11] Called 'A Dream on Inishmaan', it describes a psychic experience he identifies with the neighbourhood. Ghostly music from a stringed instrument 'tuned to a forgotten scale' enters his sleep and draws him, struggling and resisting, into a wild dance. He is

swept away in a whirlwind of notes. My breath and my thoughts and every impulse of my body, became a form of the dance, till I could not distinguish between the instruments and the rhythm and my own person or consciousness.

For a while it seemed an excitement that was filled with joy, then it grew into an ecstasy where all existence was lost in a vortex of movement. I could not think there had ever been a life beyond the whirling of the dance.

Then with a shock the ecstasy turned to an agony and rage. I struggled to free myself, but seemed only to increase the passion of the steps I moved to. When I shrieked I could only echo the notes of the rhythm.

At last with a moment of uncontrollable frenzy I broke back to consciousness and awoke.

I dragged myself trembling to the window of the cottage and looked out. The moon was glittering across the bay, and there was no sound anywhere on the island.[12]

Doubtless Yeats and Lady Gregory were pleased when they read this passage in Synge's Aran manuscript; they had urged him to 'improve' the book by adding 'more fairy belief.'[13] But although Synge had been interested for some years in – and returned later to – the study of dreams and other psychic phenomena, such a public admission from one of his evangelical background calls for special attention.[14]

About the same time he published this dream, he experienced, in Wicklow at twilight, the psychical adventure later described in his autobiography:

Before it was quite dark I looked round the edge of the field

101

and saw two immense luminous eyes looking at me from the base
of the valley. I dropped my net and caught hold of a gate in
front of me. Behind the eyes there rose a black sinister forehead.
I was fascinated. For a moment the eyes seemed to consume my
personality, then the whole valley became filled with a pageant
of movement and colour, and the opposite hillside covered itself
with ancient doorways and spires and high turrets. I did not
know where or when I was existing. At last someone spoke in
the lane behind me – it was a man going home – and I came back
to myself. The night had become quite dark and the eyes were
no longer visible, yet I recognized in a moment what had caused
the apparition – two clearings in a wood lined with white mist
divided again by a few trees which formed the eye-balls. For many
days afterwards I could not look on these fields even in daylight
without terror.[15]

Like his essay 'Under Ether,' an account of an operation in the
late '90's, Synge worked over these experiences as late as 1907 in
an attempt at some form of spiritual autobiography, but neither was
published in his lifetime.[16] Also unpublished were two other
attempts to identify and thus preserve the journeys of the spirit,
again begun in the late '90's in Paris and later revised: *Vita
Vecchia*, a series of dreams, and *Etude Morbide*, subtitled 'an
imaginary portrait.' All these works bear the same intense perception of the sudden shock of recognition, of heightened awareness
to sensations, of the transfiguration in place and time, that we see
scattered throughout his published works. But in these private
confessions, as in the dream on Inishmaan, that which is transfigured is not the observed object but the observer himself, until
he loses entirely his own self-consciousness in the ecstasy of the
cosmos. Everywhere Synge weaves through his work the 'so sudden
gust beautiful', breathtaking visions of the external world. However, in these few more personal descriptions, it is as if, in an
attempt to reconstruct the experience against a cosmic background,
Synge has had to get completely outside his own self while at the
same time recalling the primary force of the experience. He has
had to come to terms with not only the mood, but the essence, of
mysticism.

In the same way that he studied languages by attempting to write
creatively in them (sometimes with disastrous literary results), so

philosophical study and analysis accompanied this process of artistic and spiritual synthesis. Fortunately he preserved his notebooks with the random, frequently frustratingly undated or incomplete, jottings; and just as important, we can reconstruct the pattern of his reading. Further, with the help of his correspondence, especially his letters to his closest friend Stephen MacKenna (the translator of Plotinus) and later to his fiancée Molly Allgood (the Abbey actress Maire O'Neill), we can observe his frustrated attempts to incorporate these thoughts and experiences into his plays and poetry. Nor can we ignore the guideposts offered by his auto-biography: his early worship of nature as opposed to the 'man-made'; his fondness for 'the eerie and the night' and the luxury of the woods; his frank acknowledgement of wholesome sexuality and its sublimation in music and literature; his study of natural science which led to the painful separation, though only on matters of religious dogma, from his family. With this evidence it is possible to attempt a reconstruction of Synge's philosophy and perhaps come to some assessment of the spiritual values not only of his work but, of necessity, his life.

While waiting in the nursing home in December, 1897 for the operation he describes in 'Under Ether', Synge records that he read 'the great pantheist' Spinoza. That year he was also reading, among others, Thomas à Kempis, Huysmans, Keats, Wagner, de Musset, Wordsworth, Chaucer, Fiona Macleod, the Yeats–Ellis edition of William Blake, Swedenborg, Pater, Wilde, Maeterlinck, and various texts on the occult recommended by MacKenna. He apparently contemplated translating *The Little Flowers of St Francis*; he studied Shelley and Coleridge. Undoubtedly Synge embraced nature as a pantheist; writing on Aran in 1899 he was finally to put this into words: 'a human being finds a resting place only where he is in harmony with his surroundings, and is reminded that his soul and the soul of nature are of the same organization.'[17] Later he was to add, 'Universe a divine unconsciousness. Is not a twilight as vital as a human mood?'[18] For Synge the divinity of mankind and of nature were one; man's sensations are a part of the soul of the cosmos. An early draft of *When the Moon Has Set* develops this theme and man's responsibility within it:

The world is a mode of the Divine exaltation and every sane fragment of force ends in a fertile passion that is filled with joy.

103

It is the infertile excitements that are filled with death. That is the whole moral and aesthetic of the world. . . .

The worst vice is slight compared with the guiltiness of a man or woman who defies the central order of the world. . . . The only truth a wave knows is that it is going to break. The only truth a bud knows is that it is going to expand and flower. The only truth we know is that we are a flood of magnificent life the fruit of some frenzy of the earth. . . . a turmoil of life is within us. It has come from eternity and I suppose it will go on for eternity.[19]

To Synge, to be 'natural', man must accept all his sensations, and contrive 'a hierarchy of all his moods and passions.' 'No emotion is simple, and we can find the whole range of exaltation at any moment of rapture.'[20] Elsewhere he jotted down his definition of 'organic morality': 'life held to level of most inspired moments', contrasting it with what he called 'inorganic morality': 'life held to level of another [such] as Ch[ristianity] etc.'[21] We must not make the mistake of substituting 'qualities of things' (such as beauty and goodness as ends in themselves) for 'the essential things of which they are the qualities', that is 'sanity and natural perfection.' Only then will our lives become beautiful. If we seek beauty or goodness as an end our lives will become sickly; hence neither the monk's way nor the aesthete's is right. Nor, by the same token, should we deny the immediacy of our sensations or the hierarchy of moods in nature.

Nietzsche fails by seeking the sub-human and thus yoking life and joy to an hypothesis in time. A truer morality would find everything in the instant. Compare perhaps Pater noting that his views were city views rather than cosmic.[22]

The Playboy had to be set in Mayo, Synge insisted to MacKenna: 'The story – in its *essence* [the word underscored four times] – is probable given the psychic state of the locality.'[23] Old Maurya, of *Riders to the Sea*, secure in her own primeval wisdom, dismisses the young priest's attempts at comfort: 'It's little the like of him knows of the sea.' In Inishmaan there is a deeper sympathy than the church can understand between man and nature, where wonders and miracles are daily occurrences.[24] For Synge, no form of mysticism is acceptable which denies this wholeness. Writers such as Huysmans, 'a man sick with monotony', and Pierre Loti (with whom he has frequently been compared), 'tormented by the wonder of the world', both fail in their search for the permanent and infinite because they deny that full 'range of exaltation.' Loti especially is accused of embracing the 'esoteric theosophy' of Mrs Annie Besant, 'which teaches renunciation as a possible and joyful virtue.'[25] (Elsewhere Mallarmé, Baudelaire, and Villiers de l'Isle Adam are criticized for the same perversion, but Maurice Maeterlinck, whose dramas 'are directly related to the feeling of the folksong', preserves in his work 'the depth and profound humanity of the mystery which lies about us.')[26]

Synge's travels, then, became a search for, as well as the proof of, his principle of organic morality – a phrase Coleridge might have approved of.

> The religious art is a thing of the past only – a vain and foolish regret – and its place has been taken by our quite modern feeling for the beauty and mystery [of] nature . . . In my plays and topographical books I have tried to give humanity and this mysterious external world.[27]

In a very real sense, they are one and the same, and in the moods of twilight those vital cosmic forces are most likely to reveal themselves. Again and again the shock to the senses, the moment of vision, occurs during 'the two twilights', evening and dawn (usually after a rainfall), or in the quietness of the night between them. This is the time-span of his first completed play, *When the Moon Has Set*; in his last, Deirdre woos Naisi on a night with thunder coming and 'clouds coming from the west and south', she bids farewell to the little moon of Alban early one morning in the beginning of winter, and mourns her lover over a grave 'opened on a dark night.' The Tramp and the Playboy both woo with speeches of 'the dews of night, the times sweet smells do be rising, and you'd see a little shiny new moon maybe sinking on the hills.' An early title for *Etude Morbide* is 'From Twilight to Dawn.'

Such splendour can frequently cause 'a grief to the mind' when sufficiently brilliant and strikingly clear. It can lead to madness if, unsatisfied, man's moods swing too rapidly and intensely with nature's, as Synge frequently observed in his Wicklow essays:

Twilight and autumn are both full of the suggestion that we connect with death and the ending of earthly vigour, and perhaps in a country like Ireland this moment has an emphasis that is not known elsewhere. In another sense moments of supreme beauty and distinction make the impulses of the diurnal temperament jar against the impulses of the perpetual beauty which is hidden somewhere in the fountain from whence all life has come, and this jar leads us to the most profound and vain remorse anyone can experience. . . .[28]

In *The Shadow of the Glen* Nora Burke, locked into a barren and loveless marriage of her own making, sits day after day watching the season pass,

looking out from a door the like of that door, and seeing nothing but the mists rolling down the bog, and the mists again, and they rolling up the bog, and hearing nothing but the wind crying out in the bits of broken trees were left from the great storm, and the streams roaring with the rain.[29]

At such times vision is distorted, all one's senses are disturbed, man and nature alike bewildered.[30] The strength and wholeness in nature must be matched by a similar fullness and daring in man. Too much alone, Patch Darcy of *The Shadow of the Glen* runs mad in the hills, and wild Owen of *Deirdre of the Sorrows* loses his manners 'beside the Saxon bullfrogs at the head of the bog'; unloved and repressed, young Christy Mahon peeps shyly from the butt of a ditch, 'shooting out his sheep's eyes between the little twigs and leaves, and his two ears rising like a hare looking out through a gap', at a life he dares not aspire to. On the other hand, 'prepared personalities' like Deirdre, Naisi, and the old tinker woman Mary Byrne have the breadth of vision and easy sympathy with nature which can initiate action.

Nature's profound mysteries (the words resound throughout notebooks and essays) surface and are given meaning by and through the emotions of the observer, in a rhythm of completion similar to the pattern of the moments of vision evoked in his essays.

The emotions which pass through us have neither end nor

beginning, are a part of eternal sensations, and it is this almost cosmic element in the person which gives all personal art a share in the dignity of the world.

The world is an orchestra where every living thing plays one entry and then gives his place to another. We must be careful to play all the notes. It is for that we are created.

The thought was so important he repolished these passages from his notebooks, repeating them in his autobiography and in early drafts of *When the Moon Has Set*.[31] Another passage of dialogue from the same source further clarifies the pattern, again drawing, as he does so frequently, upon his training and experience with music for a suitable analogue:

A cycle of experience is the only definite unity, and when all has been passed through, and every joy and pain has been resolved in one passion of relief, the only rest that can follow is in the dissolution of the person.[32]

In his plays and essays, the sequence of sensations is clear: a sharp stab of recognition either of peculiar grief or joy almost too shocking to be borne, followed by as intense a sense of loss or loneliness, resolved in the relief or affirmation of the universality of that experience through communion with fellow man. It could be argued that in the complex movement of *Riders to the Sea* the same sequence can be traced, given greater force by the doubling up of visual and time currents on stage: the almost unbearable building-up to absolute confirmation of Maurya's grief through a series of sharply etched images where the common details of life (a walking stick, the new rope from Connemara, the white boards, a dropped stitch, even the pig with the black feet) are transfigured; Maurya's vision of double loss by the spring well when she sees into the supra-natural; her recognition that 'They're all gone now, and there isn't anything more the sea can do to me . . . It's a great rest I'll have now, and it's time surely'; concluding with the homeliness of the final exchanges between Cathleen and the mourners:

CATHLEEN. Maybe yourself and Eamon would make a coffin when the sun rises. We have fine white boards herself bought, God help her, thinking Michael would be found, and I have a new cake you can eat while you'll be working.

107

THE OLD MAN (*looking at the boards*). Are there nails with them?
CATHLEEN. There are not, Colum; we didn't think of the nails.
ANOTHER MAN. It's a great wonder she wouldn't think of the nails, and all the coffins she's seen made already.
CATHLEEN. It's getting old she is, and broken.[33]

This final 'humanizing' movement in the sequence is an essential one for Synge, and here he acknowledges his difference from Wordsworth. Synge's cosmos must be peopled; man is a necessary stage in the evolution of universal harmony and so gives meaning to creation.

> Beautiful as these Wicklow [glens] are in all seasons, when one has learned to know the people one does not love them as Wordsworth did for the sake of their home, but one feels a new glory given to the sunsets by the ragged figures they give light to.[34]

An avid photographer, Synge rarely bothered to record scenes that did not include human subjects. Finally, Nora Burke leaves her lonely cottage and cold husband not for the challenge of the road, but for the charms of the sweet-tongued stranger:

TRAMP. Come along with me now, lady of the house, and it's not my blather you'll be hearing only, but you'll be hearing the herons crying out over the black lakes, and you'll be hearing the grouse, and the owls with them, and the larks and the big thrushes when the days are warm, and it's not from the like of them you'll be hearing a talk of getting old like Peggy Cavanagh, and losing the hair off you, and the light of your eyes, but it's fine songs you'll be hearing when the sun goes up, and there'll be no old fellow wheezing the like of a sick sheep close to your ear.
NORA. I'm thinking it's myself will be wheezing that time with lying down under the Heavens when the night is cold, but you've a fine bit of talk, stranger, and it's with yourself I'll go.[35]

As has frequently been noted and can be seen most clearly in his Wicklow essays, Synge's heroes are the tramp, the herd, and the poacher – those men and women who have commerce with the night and whose senses are open to the wonders, signs and essences of the natural world. 'Man is naturally a nomad . . . and all wanderers have finer intellectual and physical perception than men who are condemned to local habitations.'[36] They are primitive in that they are childlike in their responses (notice how openly the characters in all his plays not only show their feelings but act upon them), but they are also accomplished and cunning in the measure they take of their surroundings (the blindness of Martin Doul of *The Well of the Saints* is even greater once he has been given sight; the tinkers of *The Tinker's Wedding* are overpowered only when they give in to what is for them the unnatural lore of church and town). Too frequently the artist 'lets his intellect draw the curtain of connected thought between him and the glory that is round him.' Here Synge had the advantage. Had he not wandered for years 'through the dawn of night with every nerve stiff and strained with expectation', making 'a singular acquaintance with the essences of the world'?[37] His task became the expression.of those profound psychic experiences in a natural and comprehensive form, the deliberate transfiguration of organic morality into an aesthetic creed: 'life held to the level of most inspired moments.' The hero of *Etude Morbide*, in a rare instant of comprehension, writes,

> All art that is not conceived by a soul in harmony with some mood of the earth is without value, and unless we are able to produce a myth more beautiful than nature – holding in itself a spiritual grace beyond and through the earthly – it is better to be silent.[38]

Art should never be abstract or impersonal (Synge once dismissed an English poet's work as 'anonymous, lacking the stamp of time and place.')[39] Being 'the conscious expression of his personality', as he described it in an early draft of the preface to his poems, the work of a great artist will be *unique*, carrying with it the shock of joy given by 'a thing never done before and never to be done again'; it will be *profound*, because it 'finds the inner and essential mood of the things it treats of and hence . . . is absolutely distinct and inimitable'; and, being rich, many-sided, and universal, it will be *sane*.[40]

I believe that the art we feel and recall among the greater moods of nature is the only art which is begotten of a mood in harmony with nature, of a mood then that is healthy and worthy of a place in the temple of the things that we admire. . . . The art we call decadent, or at least the more unholy portion of the art we call decadent, is not the fruit of disordered minds but rather the life of a people far from the real fount of all artistic inspiration.[41]

Great art must be rooted in the realities of time, place, and personality, while at the same time responsive to the moods of nature.

What is highest in poetry is always reached where the dreamer is leaning out to reality, or where the man of real life is lifted out of it, and in all the poets the greatest have both these elements, that is they are supremely engrossed with life, and yet with the wildness of their fancy they are always passing out of what is simple and plain.[42]

Put in terms of his famous preface, 'it is the timber of poetry that wears most surely, and there is no timber that has not strong roots among the clay and worms.' An early draft of this preface draws his aesthetic even more closely to his mystical experiences in nature: 'Twilights and exalted moments are a part of a poet's personal life, but with them the strong things of life are needed also, to show that what is tender is not weak.'[43] And elsewhere the single statement, 'where would we put Dante's Paradise if Hell was not below it?'[44] Put in theatrical terms, Christy Mahon is given his most poetic and fanciful dialogue when pinned to the ground and his most extravagant speeches when hot and sweaty from a mule race; the reaffirmation of Martin Doul's idealism leads him to a stoning and a certain death; the dream and the reality, the romantic and the Rabelaisian, do not restrain each other but develop to individual climaxes side by side. Synge's most difficult problem in writing *Deirdre of the Sorrows* was in trying to decide what 'fundamental realities of life' lay behind the 'story that is foretold.' 'Poetic subject matter' is a deadly sin;[45] 'Utopian' or romantic work is unsatisfying, because 'it is only the catastrophes of life that give substance and power to the tragedy and humour which are the two

110

poles of art.'[46] 'Atmosphere should be in the essence';[47] setting, dialogue, character and subject must be one.

On reading Anatole France, one of the few contemporaries whom he admired, Synge once commented:

It is interesting to notice how many of the more important writers of the last quarter of a century have used dialogue for their medium, and thus kept up a direct relation with the spoken language, and the life of those who speak it. How much more effective, for instance, has been the varied treatment of dialogue by Maeterlinck, Oscar Wilde, Anatole France, Ibsen and others, from any elaborate prose produced during the same period.[48]

It was inevitable that he should choose dialogue; drama, he remarked to an Australian journalist, is a better form than the novel. 'You get rid of so much waste description and analysis that you don't want.'[49] What he did want was to capture the essence of place and character in a striking manner which could reflect the peculiar intensity of life 'held to its most inspired moments', those 'so sudden gust[s] beautiful'; atmosphere and action must be developed together. None of his characters must be other than unique, strong in the presentation of personality, true to his own inner responses. They are boldly drawn: 'types' for Synge did not mean either caricatures or 'type-casting', but did mean the memorable.[50] When we turn to the plays, we find that every character is strikingly individual in thought and action, creating little vignettes that linger in the mind long after the performance or reading is over – the Tramp in *The Shadow of the Glen* stitching his coat while muttering the 'de Profundis' under his breath; high-spirited young girls carrying in the Saint's bell, cloak and water-can in Act I of *The Well of the Saints*; Mary and Martin Doul 'hiding', clearly visible to the Saint and villagers in Act III of the same play; the Priest in *The Tinker's Wedding* sharing a sup of porter by firelight with the disreputable Mary Byrne and her son. I can think of no 'minor' characters or empty action in any of his mature work. All his people are fully conscious and aware, embarked on the great adventure of self-discovery.

Their language too is full-blooded and peculiar, like Hopkins', 'mouthed to flesh-burst.' Synge's painstaking reworking of each

111

speech was not embroidery, but an effort to catch the richness and truth of personality and imagination.[51] 'In moments of spiritual excitement the voice has a peculiar intonation which is the element of all power and literature,' he wrote in his notebook, and elsewhere, 'Perhaps the language of the real person cannot be very far from the language we speak in dreams.'[52] His delight in the coinages and copiousness overheard on the roads or – and perhaps at last we might put paid to the image of Synge at the keyhole – in the houses of Wicklow, Kerry and Mayo was pleasure in the folk-imagination of the people who uttered it. 'I do not know that there is anything blessed in anaemia,' he once wrote to MacKenna.[53] Here is *tasty* speech, to be chewed and loved and remembered with a shock of delighted recognition. It spirals, swoops, turns sharply, reaches:

> Amn't I after seeing the love-light of the star of knowledge shining from her brow, the hearing words would put you thinking on the holy Brigid speaking to the infant saints, and now she'll be turning again, and speaking hard words to me, like an old woman with a spavindy ass she'd have urging on a hill.[54]

It sharpens our senses:

> There's the sound of one of them twittering yellow birds do be coming in the spring-time from beyond the sea, and there'll be a fine warmth now in tne sun, and a sweetness in the air, the way it'll be a grand thing to be sitting here quiet and easy, smelling the things growing up, and budding from the earth.[55]

Or it mourns:

> Woods of Cuan, woods of Cuan . . . It's seven years we've had a life was joy only and this day we're going west, this day we're facing death maybe, and death should be a poor untidy thing, though it's a queen that dies.[56]

But always, it is a song of praise to the grandeur and glory of the world orchestra in which man plays his part.

'The two subjects on which all our glory is constructed are the facts of love and death,' the hero of *When the Moon Has Set* argues.

To Stephen MacKenna, who insisted on special subject-matter for drama, Synge is even more definite: 'I think squeamishness is a disease, and that Ireland will gain if Irish writers deal manfully, directly and *decently* with the entire reality of life.'[57] Law-breaker and law-maker are both needful to society and hence to drama; so also is the honest presentation of sensuality and all forms of physical beauty.

All art is perhaps an expression [of] a trebly refined and purged growth of the joy of sensual love or the sorrow of desire as all religion in so far as it is an ecstasy rather than a philosophy is a growth of the sensual love nourished in the sentiments.[58]

In his autobiography Synge explores the role that sexuality has played in his own life: 'I saw in one hour that both nature and women were alive with indescribable radiance – with beauty.'[59] Here, in *Vita Vecchia* and even more overtly in *Etude Morbide*,[60] he anatomizes his own growing awareness of the relation between music, dreams, and the powerful forces of the sexual in women and nature:

I joined an amateur orchestra [while a student at Trinity College], which gave me unusual pleasure. The collective passion produced by a band working together with one will and ideal is unlike any other exaltation . . . We played the *Jupiter Symphony* of Mozart. It was in an academy and a Jewess was playing at the desk before me. No other emotion that I have received was quite so puissant or complete. A slight and altogether subconscious avidity of sex wound and wreathed itself in the extraordinary beauty of the movement, not unlike the sexual element that exists in all really fervent ecstasies of faith. . . . I found the mysterious mansion I had dreamed, I played with morbid assiduity. I remember particularly the long blue days of a June that I spent looking out over the four strings of my violin into the filling leaves and white erect florescence of a chestnut and a wilderness of plants beneath it that crushed and strangled each other in a green and silent frenzy of expression. . . . One is lost in a blind tempest that wails round one with always beautiful passion, the identity is merged in a . . . symmetrical joy, cathedrals build themselves about one with the waves of purple storm, yet one remains sane and a man.[61]

113

His Kerry and Aran essays relate with candour the attractiveness of the women:

> These women are before convention and share many things with the women of Paris or London who have freed themselves by a desperate personal effort from moral bondage of lady-like persons. . . . I have found a couple that have been turned in on themselves by some circumstance of their lives and seem to sum up in the expressions of their blue grey eyes the whole external symphony of the sky and seas. They have wildness and humour and passion kept in continual subjection by the reverence for life and the sea that is inevitable in this place.[62]

In his notebooks he wonders

> what in the new literature I have dreamed of will be the conception of love for on it will depend a good deal of the fortunes of humanity. . . . In what way will they create for us a romance of reality. . . . Most important of all – How will they rescue love – the word is not too strong – from the French?[63]

In his plays he set about to do so, and the result was the storm of protest over *The Shadow of the Glen*. Synge was accused of casting a slur on Irish womanhood, of decadence and cynicism, untruth and unpatriotism. Responding to Stephen MacKenna's mild objection, he once again asserted his plea for wholeness and sincerity in art as in life:

> Heaven forbid that we should ever have a morbid sex-obsesed [sic] drama in Ireland, not because we have any peculiarly blessed sanctity which I utterly deny – see percentage of lunatics in Ireland and causes thereof – but because it is bad drama and is played out. On the French stage the sex-element of life is given without the other balancing elements; on the Irish stage the people you agree with want the other elements without sex. I restored the sex-element to its natural place, and the people were so surprised they saw the sex only.[64]

The Well of the Saints went further still, by sympathetically presenting, among other things, the dangers of frustrated passions

114

and the wrong-headedness of denial and renunciation. Finally, in *The Playboy of the Western World* and *Deirdre of the Sorrows* he celebrated the glory of a love returned and the hierarchy of passions awakened.

It is in many ways unfortunate that Synge's last plays also dwelt on the fact of death, for to many critics this has seemed proof positive of morbidity.[65] But Synge did not invent the troubles of Deirdre and Naisi, any more than he would deny the cruelty that is inherent in nature alongside the beauty, or the brevity of man's phase in the cycle. 'No one pretends to ignore the bitterness of disease and death. It is an immense infinite horror, and the more we learn to set the real value on the vitality of his life the more we will dread death.'[66] The hero of *Vita Vecchia* is haunted by

the briefness of my world. It brings me at times a passionate thirst for the fulfilment of every passive or active capacity of my person. It seems a crime that I should go home and sleep in trite sheets while heaven and earth slip away from me for ever.[67]

On Aran,

the black curragh working slowly through this world of grey, and the soft hissing of the rain gave me one of the moods in which we realise with immense distress the short moment we have left us to experience all the wonder and beauty of the world.[68]

Synge once told MacKenna that 'all the sadness he had in the thought of death was that while he lay there cloistered the seasons would come and go and he know nothing of it at all.'[69] Death is, like love, a great intensifier (might even, through illness, lead as it did with Keats to hypersensitivity and ever greater awareness). Synge recalls how as a child, a death in the family was 'only strong enough to evoke the full luxury of the woods.'[70] Perhaps final oneness with nature and the cosmos can only be achieved when, like Deirdre, one selects time and place, or, like Maurya, recognizes death's limitations. Consider the danger of riding the waves:

At one moment, as we went down into the furrow, green waves curled and arched themselves above me; then in an instant I was

115

flung up into the air and could look down on the heads of the
rowers, as if we were sitting on a ladder, or out across a forest
of white crests to the black cliff of Inishmaan. The men seemed
excited and uneasy, and I thought for a moment that we were
likely to be swamped. In a little while, however, I realised the
capacity of the curragh to raise its head among the waves, and
the motion became strangely exhilarating. Even, I thought, if
we were dropped into the blue chasm of the waves, this death,
with the fresh sea saltness in one's teeth, would be better than
most deaths one is likely to meet.[71]

The fact of death differs only by degrees from other sharp pangs
of loss or desolation 'that is mixed everywhere with the supreme
beauty of the world.'[72] 'We must be careful to play all the notes; it
is for that we are created. If we play well we are not exorbitantly
wretched.'[73]

Finally, Synge found nature, love, and the entire spectrum of
emotions in his relationship with Molly Allgood. In late December
1906, after a hard spell of work on *The Playboy*, he wrote to her of
the completeness of their love:

You feel as fully as anyone can feel all the poetry and mystery
of the nights we are out in – like that night a week ago when we
came down from Rockbrook with the pale light of Dublin shining
behind the naked trees till we seemed almost to come out of
ourselves with the wonder and beauty of it all. Divine moments
like that are infinitely precious to us both as people and as artists
I with my writing and you with your acting, and by reading what
is greatest in poetry or hearing what is greatest in Music – things
like the Messiah – one trains one's soul, as a singer trains his
voice, to respond to and understand the great moments of our
own lives or of the outside world. I think people who feel these
things – people like us – have a profound joy in love, that the
ordinary run of people do not easily reach. They love with all
their hearts – as we do – but their hearts perhaps, have not all
the stops that you and I have found in ours. The worst of it is
that we have the same openness to profound pain – of mind I
mean – as we have to profound joy, but please Heaven we shall
have a few years of divine love and life together and that is all I
suppose any one need expect.[74]

116

'We do wrong,' the hero of *Vita Vecchia* concludes his story,

> to seek a foundation for ecstasy in philosophy or the hidden things of the spirit – if there is spirit – for when life is at its simplest, with nothing beyond or before it, the mystery is greater than we can endure. Every leaf and flower [and] insect is full of deeper wonder than any sign the cabbalists have invented.[75]

To seek out and create a life and art held to the 'level of most inspired moments' is to acknowledge first the mystery of man in an infinity of space, place, and the senses. Did Synge and Joyce compare epiphanies when they met in Paris? We shall probably never know. Perhaps the key to Synge's universe was unwittingly offered by Yeats, even before the two poets met. For we do know that in the Yeats/Ellis edition of the works of William Blake the young student in Paris read the following lines which epitomize his own nature mysticism (I transpose them here in the interests of rhetoric):

> For man has closed himself up, till he sees all things thro' narrow chinks of his cavern.
>
> *   *   *
>
> If the doors of perception were cleansed every thing would appear as it is, infinite.[76]

NOTES

(Quotations from Synge's work in this essay come from the four volume edition *J. M. Synge: Collected Works* (London: Oxford University Press, 1962-8), hereafter cited as *C.W.* The volumes are as follows: *I. Poems* (1962), ed. Robin Skelton; II, *Prose* (1966), ed. Alan Price; III, *Plays: Book I* (1968), ed. Ann Saddlemyer; IV, *Plays: Book II* (1968), ed. Ann Saddlemyer.)

1 *C.W.* II, 282. Synge's projected volume *In West Kerry*, on which he was working in 1907 and 1908, was based on three essays published in *The Shanachie* in 1907 and additional material from his notebooks; it was organized but not finished at his death. Cf. a similar experience recorded in his Wicklow notebooks, C.W. II, 194-95.

2 *C.W.* II, 129-30.
3 *C.W.* II, 75.
4 *C.W.* II, 73.
5 *C.W.* II, 113.
6 *C.W.* II, 73.
7 *C.W.* II, 108-110.
8 *C.W.* II, 120.
9 *C.W.* II, 97 note 1. See also Edward Stephens, *My Uncle John,* ed. Andrew Carpenter (London: Oxford University Press, 1974), pp. 121-22 and p. 50.
10 Gerard Manly Hopkins, 'Moonrise'; Virginia Woolf, *Mrs. Dalloway* (1947), p. 36.
11 Pamela Colman ('Pixie') Smith published *The Green Sheaf,* 1903-04; she had earlier worked with Jack Yeats on his *Broadsheets* and later was to be responsible for the designs of the new Waite Tarot pack. Synge's dream appeared in *The Green Sheaf* no. 2, 1903, and was reprinted in *The Gael,* March 1904.
12 *C.W.* II, 100.
13 On 1 October, 1901, Lady Gregory wrote from Coole, where she and Yeats had been reading the first three parts of *The Aran Islands,* 'the book would be greatly improved by the addition of some more fairy belief.'
14 Synge's family acknowledged the second sight of Harry Stephens (Synge's brother-in-law), but even Stephens disowned mysticism and the occult. cf. *My Uncle John,* p. 68. As early as 1892, Synge recorded dreams in his diary; in 1897 he was discussing works on the occult with Stephen MacKenna, and according to a letter from MacKenna in 1907, he was once again studying the subject.
15 *C.W.* II, 10. In *My Uncle John,* pp. 129-30 which quotes a slightly different version of this experience, Stephens cites evidence for a date of June 1899; Synge had evidently placed the experience further back in time, probably when revising his autobiography in 1907. See also *My Uncle John,* p. 136.
16 See *C.W.* II, 39-43, especially p. 42: 'I seemed to traverse whole epochs of desolation and bliss. All secrets were open before me, and simple as the universe to its God. Now and then something recalled my physical life, and I smiled at what seemed a moment of sickly infancy. At other times I felt I might return to earth, and laughed aloud to think what a god I should be among men. For there could be no more terror in my life. I was a light, a joy.'
17 Wherever possible, all quotations from the manuscripts bear the number assigned by Trinity College Dublin Library. This notebook, in use in 1899 and later, is MS. 4384. MS.4389 speaks of 'a pantheistic emotion which is spread so widely before the path we follow that it seems the inevitable and ultimate mood of all art.'
18 MS. 4392.
19 Quoted in *C.W.* III, 168 note 2, Cf. p. 164 note 2 and *C.W.* II, 24.
20 *C.W.* III, 168 note 2.
21 MS. 4384. Cf. *C.W.* III, 280.

22 MS. 4393.
23 'Synge to MacKenna: The Mature Years,' ed. Ann Saddlemyer, in *Irish Renaissance,* edd. Robin Skelton and David R. Clark (Dublin: Dolmen Press, 1965), p. 75. Compare this passage describing an evening in West Kerry: 'I turned up a sharp, green hill, and came out suddenly on the broken edge of a cliff. The effect was wonderful. The Atlantic was right underneath; then I could see the sharp rocks of several uninhabited islands, a mile of two off, the Tearaught further away, and, on my left, the whole northern edge of this island curving round towards the west, with a steep, heathery face, a thousand feet high. The whole sight of wild islands and sea was as clear and cold and brilliant as what one sees in a dream, and alive with the singularly severe glory that is in the character of this place.' (*C.W.* II, 248.)
24 *C.W.* II, 128-29.
25 'Loti and Huysmans,' *The Speaker* (18 April 1903), pp. 57-58. This passage is omitted in *C.W.* II, 395.
26 MS. 4382.
27 *C.W.* II, 351.
28 *C.W.* II, 200.
29 *C.W.* III, 49.
30 See 'Glencree', *C.W.* II, 234-35 and 'The Oppression of the Hills', *C.W* II, 209-12.
31 *C.W.* III, 174-76; see also II, 3.
32 *C.W.* III, 176; cf. II, 14.
33 *C.W.* III, 25.
34 *C.W.* II, 228 note 1; cf. also II, 196.
35 *C.W.* III, 57.
36 *C.W.* II, 195-96.
37 *C.W.* II, 9-10.
38 *C.W.* II, 35. Although we differ considerably in our interpretations, I agree with Dr. Jeanne Flood ('The Pre-Aran Writing of J. M. Synge,' *Eire-Ireland,* V. 3 (Autumn 1970), pp. 63-80) that we must approach any autobiographical intent with caution. An article by Professor Gerard Le Blanc, 'J. M. Synge in Paris,' *France Ireland: Literary Relations* (Paris: Editions Universitaires, Publications de l'Université de Lille III, 'Cahiers Irlandais' no. 2/3, 1974, pp. 191-213) throws interesting light on Synge's early literary experiences in France.
39 Quoted by Louis Esson, 'J. M. Synge: a Personal Note,' in *Fellowship* (Melbourne, Australia), VII, 9 (April 1921), pp. 138-41.
40 *C.W.* II, 349-51; cf. III, xxviii, 'the eternal problem . . . finding a universal expression for the particular virtues and ideas of the personality of the artist himself.'
41 MS. 4349.
42 *C.W.* II, 347.
43 MS. 4364.
44 MS. 4411.
45 See also his letter to MacKenna, *Irish Renaissance,* pp. 66-68.
46 *C.W.* II, 350.
47 MS. 4396. In MS. 4392, Synge analyzes the relationship between 'unity

119

of atmosphere' and 'the strength of the action' in certain plays by Shakespeare and others, including Ibsen.

48   *C.W.* II, 396.
49   Esson, p. 140. See Ann Saddlemyer, ' "A Share in the Dignity of the World": J. M. Synge's Aesthetic Theory,' in *The World of W. B. Yeats* (Dublin: Dolmen Press, 1965), p. 246 for his rating of the dialogue of certain authors.
50   At one time he contemplated writing a series of articles on 'Types of Irishmen' for the *Manchester Guardian.* See *Letters to Molly: J. M. Synge to Maire O'Neill,* ed. Ann Saddlemyer (Cambridge, Mass: Harvard University Press, 1971), p. 187; *C.W.* II, 284 note, 287, 326 and 102 note.
51   During rehearsal he refused to alter certain words once they were established within the fabric of the play, insisting on their 'atmosphere' for the locality, Esson, p. 141; cf. also *C.W.* III, xxiv.
52   MS. 4382. In the same notebook he wrote: 'in rapt moment we do not think in style like Mallarmé's.'
53   'Synge to MacKenna,' p. 67.
54   *The Playboy of the Western World,* II; *C.W.* IV, 126-27.
55   *The Well of the Saints,* III; *C.W.* III, 132.
56   *Deirdre of the Sorrows,* II; *C.W.* IV, 239.
57   'Synge to MacKenna,' pp. 67-68.
58   *When the Moon Has Set,* C.W. III, 278.
59   *C.W.* II, 13.
60   See especially the 'vision' described in *Etude Morbide. C.W.* II, 34.
61   *C.W.* II, 14.
62   *C.W.* II, 143 note; see also pp. 54, 113 note, 237, 238 and 252.
63   'A Share in the Dignity of the World', p. 252.
64   'Synge to MacKenna', p. 67, includes a variation on this letter; the final draft Synge sent to MacKenna is in the Lilly Library, Indiana University, with whose permission it is here reproduced.
65   A fine rebuttal of this charge of morbidity is given by Sean McMahon in 'Clay and Worms', *Eire-Ireland,* V, 4 (Winter, 1970), pp. 116-34.
66   *C.W.* III, 176 note.
67   *C.W.* II, 20-21.
68   *C.W.* II, 139.
69   *The Journal and Letters of Stephen MacKenna,* ed. E. R. Dodds (London: Constable, 1936), p. 114.
70   *C.W.* II, 7.
71   *C.W.* II, 97.
72   *C.W.* II, 240.
73   *C.W.* II, 24.
74   *Letters to Molly,* p. 81.
75   *C.W.* II, 24.
76   William Blake, *The Marriage of Heaven and Hell.*

JOYCE'S USE OF THE ANGLO-IRISH DIALECT OF ENGLISH

RICHARD WALL

The most neglected major element of James Joyce's style is his use of the Anglo-Irish dialect of English. It is rather odd that there should be Gaelic and German lexicons for *Finnegans Wake*, while his extensive use of his native dialect in his works is virtually ignored.[1] Irish readers naturally tend to take his use of the dialect for granted. Non-Irish readers tend to do the same because of its apparent proximity to standard English. Joyce appears to have anticipated such responses; he felt compelled in a number of his letters to draw attention to and explain Anglo-Irish words and phrases, which he used to extend or reinforce the meaning of his text. If the many errors in published criticism are any indication, the thought that the dialect might prove a barrier to those who are unfamiliar with it does not appear to have occurred to many critics. These errors suggest that the problems caused by Joyce's use of the dialect are serious and widespread. They range from incomplete understanding to complete misunderstanding of parts of his works. Like every other element of his style, he selected the Anglo-Irish dialect with care and used it with precision. It demands far more attention and understanding than it appears to be getting. The purpose of this paper is to provide an outline of his use of the dialect and illustrate some of the pitfalls it poses for the unsuspecting.

A superficial examination of Joyce's works reveals that his use of the Anglo-Irish dialect is not uniform. It is more prominent in *Ulysses* and *Finnegans Wake* than in *Dubliners* and *A Portrait of the Artist as a Young Man*. Even within the works his use of the dialect is not uniform. It is more prominent in 'Cyclops' than in 'Scylla and Charybdis'; more prominent in 'Anna Livia' than in 'Shem'. The fact that it is completely absent from *Chamber Music* and massively employed in *Finnegans Wake* gives some idea of the

121

extent to which his interest in the dialect increased as he matured and his style changed.

The discontinuity which has been noted between the bulk of Joyce's poems and his other works is also reflected in the absence of the Anglo-Irish dialect from *Chamber Music* and its scarcity in *Pomes Penyeach*. Given the ease with which Anglo-Irish speech can be married to song, its absence from *Chamber Music*, which he described as 'a suite of songs,' is strange (*Letters* I, 67).[2] This may be a reflection of his early desire to avoid sounding too Irish, or, more likely, he may have felt the dialect to be incompatible with his attempt to evoke through 'elegant and antique phrase' the age of Dowland, Holinshed and Purchas (*CP* 35). In 1906 he said that he disliked the title *Chamber Music* because it was 'too complacent' (*Letters* II, 182). He added that he would 'prefer a title which to a certain extent repudiated the book, without altogether disparaging it.' In 1927 a common Dublin street-cry, 'pomes penyeach,' provided him with such a title for his second volume of poems. The only Anglo-Irish word in his *Collected Poems*, apart from the occasional place name, is 'Tilly,' the third title[3] given to the first poem of *Pomes Penyeach* (*CP* 47). The meaning of the word, which is derived from the Irish word *tuilleadh* (added measure),[4] is well understood, but the connection between the title and the poem is not. In *Finnegans Wake* he uses the Anglo-Irish diminutive suffix *een* and the Dublin pronunciation of dozen in his hint of the meaning of tilly: 'A bakereen's dusind' (212.21). The term is most often used in the measurement of milk, a fact which is reflected in the description of the old milkwoman in *Ulysses*: 'She poured again a measureful and a tilly' (13). 'Tilly' is an appropriate title for the extra (thirteenth) poem in the collection and also for a poem about a drover and his herd of cattle. However, Joyce's purpose in placing the extra poem at the beginning of the collection rather than the end is not clear.

There is an obvious pun in the title of Joyce's 1912 verse broadside, *Gas from a Burner* (*CW* 242). Gas is the most common synonym for fun in Ireland; the word is used in this sense in *Finnegans Wake*: 'great gas with fun-in-the-corner' (577.07–08). There is a less obvious pun in the title given to the broadside in *Finnegans Wake*: 'gash from a burner! ' (93.11). Gash is an Anglo-Irish term for a concluding, ornamental, curved flourish made with a pen.[5] There is internal evidence that the pun on this obscure term is deliberate. The original of the document known as the 'Tiberiast duplex' in 'The Book of Kells' section of the work appeared at first glance to be completely devoid of punctuation, but when carefully examined it was discovered to be 'pierced butnot punctured . . . by numerous stabs and foliated gashes made by a pronged instrument. These paper wounds . . . were gradually and correctly understood to mean stop' (124.01–04).

Redundancy is a prominent feature of Anglo-Irish speech. Its extensive use in *Dubliners* would have made it difficult for Joyce to achieve 'a style of scrupulous meanness,' which he felt his subject required (*Letters* II, 134). It is sparingly but effectively used throughout for the purpose of verisimilitude. At the beginning of 'Counterparts,' the reader is informed that Mr Alleyne has 'a piercing North of Ireland accent' (86). The accent is not reproduced, but the reader is later reminded of Mr Alleyne's origin and accent through his use of one word, 'mind' (heed), as he berates Farrington: 'Do you mind me, now?' (87). There is only one attempt to represent Irish pronunciation of English words phonetically in the work. In 'A Mother' Mrs Kearney, in her anger at Mr Fitzpatrick, is sorely tempted to ask 'who is the *Cometty*, [committee] pray?' (141).

In 'The Dead' the differences between the speech of Gabriel, Lily, and Gabriel's wife Gretta, underscore in a subtle way class and regional differences. Gabriel Conroy is an educated and well-travelled Dubliner; his speech is standard English, and he smiles when Lily, who is a Dublin caretaker's daughter, gives his surname three syllables (177). Her bitter retort to one of his innocent questions reflects her class: 'The men that is now is only all palaver and what they can get out of you' (178). Gretta's speech, which contains a number of phrases literally translated from Irish, reflects the fact that she is from Galway. She told Michael Furey that he would 'get his death in the rain' (221). In Irish one does not die, one 'gets death' (*bás d'fhagháil*). Speech is also used in *Exiles* to reflect class differences. Bertha, the old servant of the Rowan family, uses a characteristic Anglo-Irish sentence to describe her master's literary activity: 'Up half the night he does be' (16). The words are English, but the syntax is Irish; it is a literal translation of *Ina shuidhe leath na h-oidche a bhíonn sé.* When the Irish adopted or were forced to adopt English, they discovered that one of its defects was its lack of a habitual present tense of the verb 'to be'. They

123

rectified this by simply translating their own *bíonn sé* (he does be). Despite the usefulness of this verb form, its use is inhibited. Educated Irish people, unless they are being ironic, avoid its use, because it is considered a mark of uneducated speech. It is unlikely that one of Bertha's class would ever use or even understand an Anglo-Irish phrase used by Robert Hand. When he loftily announces that he is 'a descendant of the dark foreigners' (43), he displays his knowledge of an ancient Irish distinction between two sets of Scandinavian invaders: the *Dubh-Ghall* (Dark-Foreigners, Danish) and the *Finn-Ghall* (Fair-Foreigners, Norwegian). In one of his letters to Harriet Shaw Weaver, Joyce indicated his use of *Dubh-Ghall* in *Finnegans Wake* and explained its meaning (SL 297).

The care with which Joyce uses the Anglo-Irish vocabulary can be seen in his use of the words chapel and church in *Dubliners*. In Joyce's time Catholic places of worship were usually called chapels, while Protestant places of worship were usually called churches. This practice can even be seen on the maps of the period, which distinguish between 'Church' and 'R.C. Chapel.'[6] Eliza in 'The Sisters' and Farrington's son in 'Counterparts' use the word chapel for Catholic Church (18, 97). However, the more well-to-do and pretentious Catholics in Dublin tended to call their places of worship churches, a fact which is reflected in Joyce's description of Mrs Kiernan in 'Grace': 'she still hurried to the chapel door whenever a wedding was reported and, seeing the bridal pair, recalled with vivid pleasure how she had passed out of the Star of the Sea Church in Sandymount, leaning on the arm of a jovial well-fed man' (156). The Catholic Church less than a mile away from Sandymount in working-class Ringsend was (and still is) invariably called St Patrick's Chapel.

From the point of view of this paper, the most interesting story in *Dubliners* is 'A Little Cloud'. It contains Joyce's earliest attempts to exploit the resources of the Anglo-Irish dialect to add to or reinforce the meaning of his work. The central character has an odd name, Little Chandler. Chandler is an Anglo-Irish term for maggot, most common perhaps among butchers and fishermen. Little Chandler, a meek clerk in the King's Inns, is, metaphorically, a little maggot. The hint which is given by his name is reinforced in the description of him on his way home from work: 'He picked his way deftly through all that minute vermin-like life of [Henrietta

Street]' (71). He is patronized by an obnoxious, returned emigrant, Ignatius Gallaher. As part of his exposure of Gallaher's crassness, Joyce has him display his ignorance of the well-known Gaelic phrase, '*deoc an doruis*' (sic), which is common to Anglo-Scottish and Anglo-Irish speech. It means parting drink, literally 'drink of the door,' but Gallaher believes it is 'good vernacular for a small whisky' (80).

The first and last obvious examples of Anglo-Irish dialect in *Dubliners* are perfect traps for Freudians. In 'The Sisters' the uncle explains to old Cotter that the dead priest 'had a great wish for' the boy narrator of the story (10). In using the phrase 'great wish,' the uncle does not mean 'great desire'; he means 'great esteem'. The phrase is a loose translation of the Irish phrase *meas mór*.[7] Near the end of 'The Dead,' there is an emotionally charged conversation between Gabriel and Gretta Conroy. In her response to his leading statement, 'I suppose you were in love with this Michael Furey,' she uses, as people do under stress, a stock phrase: 'I was great with him at that time' (220). The phrase 'I was great with' is the exact equivalent of a common Irish phrase, *Bhí mé mór le* (I was great [friendly] with). The phrase is devoid of sexual connotations in Irish and Anglo-Irish. Nevertheless, Zack Bowen, in his recently published book on Joyce's musical allusions, sees in Gretta's use of the phrase a 'suggestion that there was fertility in the liaison between her and Furey.'[8] A close reading of the text and an awareness of the connotations of the phrase 'I was great with' would surely suggest that this is not what Joyce meant at all.

Joyce's attitude towards titles, quoted above, is reflected in his substitution of *A Portrait of the Artist as a Young Man* for *Stephen Hero*, as the title of his first novel. By insisting on the importance of the last four words of the title, he distracted attention from the word 'artist', which is the most ambiguous and important in the title. Joyce appears to have selected it because, in addition to its use in the conventional sense, it is the most common synonym in Anglo-Irish speech for 'rogue'. There is an obvious connection between the hint given in the title and Stephen's 'arms' at the end of the novel (247). A rogue needs 'cunning', and 'exile' is his version of the midnight flit (247). For much of his time at Belvedere College his life is 'a tissue of subterfuge and falsehood' (98). What is implicit in the title of *A Portrait* is made very explicit in *Ulysses*. As Stephen walks along Sandymount Strand, he imagines his father asking sarcastically: 'Did you see anything of your artist brother Stephen lately?' (38).

Within *A Portrait* Joyce uses the Anglo-Irish dialect in much the same way and for the same reasons as he does in *Dubliners*. Near the end of the first chapter, Thunder explains that the boys who ran away from school did so 'Because they had fecked cash out of the rector's room' (40). It is clear from the context that 'fecked' means stolen, a fact which is confirmed by Stephen musing: 'But that was stealing.' Later a different and more sinister explanation for the boys' flight is given by Athy; they ran away because they were caught 'Smugging' (42). This is greeted with silence: 'Stephen . . . wanted to ask someone about it. What did that mean about the smugging in the square? Why did the five fellows out of the higher line run away for that?' The reader's attention is drawn to this dialect word, but, because Stephen does not dare ask, its precise meaning is not revealed, although it obviously means some form of homosexual activity. Brendan O Hehir incorrectly suggests that the word is of possible Irish etymology, but his explanations give no clue to its meaning.[9] It means 'To toy amorously in secret,' and it is also an English dialect word.[10]

Stephen's preoccupation with language is bound up with his sensitivity to the fact that Anglo-Irish speech is not the same as English speech, and the fact that the English language is a relatively recent acquisition of the bulk of the Irish people. This is evident in some of his thoughts during his battle of wits with the English priest, who is Dean of Studies:

> The language in which we are speaking is his before it is mine. How different are the words *home, Christ, ale, master* on his lips and on mine! I cannot speak or write these words without unrest of spirit. His language, so familiar and so foreign, will always be for me an acquired speech. I have not made or accepted its words. My voice holds them at bay. My soul frets in the shadow of his language. (189)

His awareness of some of the sources of the Anglo-Irish dialect is evident in his response to the speech of the rustic Davin, which, he notes, contains 'rare phrases of Elizabethan English' and 'quaintly turned versions of Irish idioms' (195).

The dispute between Stephen and the English priest over the

126

meaning and distribution of the word 'tundish' (188, 251) is the result of a prominent feature of the Anglo-Irish dialect; its preservation of a number of rare or obsolete English words and phrases. These words appear occasionally in Joyce's works, from 'mitching' (playing truant) at the beginning of *Dubliners* to 'forenenst' (opposite) at the end of *Finnegans Wake* (*D* 21, *FW* 626.22). In the latter they are frequently used in puns, as in 'the possing of the showers' (51.02). Possing (very wet) is an obsolete English word still current in Ireland. The rare or obsolete English greeting 'good morrow' is still heard in Ireland. It appears as 'morrow' in *Ulysses* (39), and in *Finnegans Wake* there is a pun on the greeting. 'Gomorrha' (579.23) is the Biblical city of that name, and also, as the context clearly indicates, a phonetic spelling of the usual pronunciation of the phrase. Rare or obsolete Anglo-Irish words and phrases also appear occasionally in Joyce's works. Few Irish people now use or even know the meaning of the word 'wirrasthrue' (sorrowful), or the phrase 'wet and dry' (constant). The former, which appears in *Stephen Hero*, is a phonetic spelling of the Irish phrase *A Mhuire is truagh* (O Mary it is a pity or sorrow), while the latter, which appears in *Gas from a Burner* and *Ulysses*, has its origin in constant work of the kind not interrupted by the notoriously fickle Irish weather (*SH* 113, *CW* 243, *U* 199). Of two annotations of *Ulysses* published recently, one by Don Gifford and Robert J. Seidman ignores the phrase 'wet and dry,'[11] while the other by Patrick A. McCarthy provides a wildly inaccurate explanation based on the theory of humours.[12]

The incidence of Anglo-Irish dialect in each episode of *Ulysses* reflects the milieu of the episode. In 'Scylla and Charybdis' there is very little in the lofty discussion of Shakespeare by the *literati* of Dublin in the National Library. The incidence increases with a change in tone heralded by the appearance of Mulligan, who uses the dialect ironically. He adopts a 'querulous brogue' (199) as he keens or wails coarse parodies of Synge: *'Pogue mahone! Acushla machree!* (Kiss my arse! Pulse of my heart!) It's destroyed we are from this day! It's destroyed we are surely! ' (205). The Irish here is Mulligan's; the English is adapted from *Riders to the Sea*.[13] When Joyce wrote the episode, he had a long-standing contempt for 'peasant plays' (*U* 203), and for those who would base their art on 'The Folk' (*CW* 42, *U* 12). The conversation of the denizens of a Dublin pub, as they discuss more earthly matters in 'Cyclops', is larded with Anglo-Irish words and phrases. They range from the gentle 'mavourneen's' (my darling's, 293) at the beginning to the blunt 'Arrah, sit down on the parliamentary side of your arse' (Look, sit down and behave yourself, 342) at the end. Their conversation also contains fourteen common Irish words, names, phrases or slogans of the kind with which some Irish nationalists like to pepper their speech: *'Sraid na Bretaine Bheag'* (Little Britain Street, 316); *'Raimeis'* (Nonsense, 326); *'Bi i dho husht'* (Be quiet, 299); and *'Lamh Dearg Abu'* (Red Hand to Victory, 325).

The first Anglo-Irish word in *Ulysses* is a very simple and common one. When Mulligan cannot find his handkerchief on which to wipe his razor, he cries 'Scutter' (4). Gifford and Seidman explain that the word means 'a scurrying or bustling about,'[14] even though it is obvious from the context that this is not what Mulligan means. As every Irish child knows, the word means diarrhoea. Such ignorance of Anglo-Irish vocabulary is inexcusable in a guide to Joyce. The meaning of scutter also eluded Joseph Campbell and Henry Morton Robinson in their guide to *Finnegans Wake*. They are aware of the defecation theme in the story of Buckley and the Russian General, but they miss an obvious example when they paraphrase 'Scutterer of guld' (340.01) as 'Scatterer of Gold! '[15] The failure of Gifford and Seidman to check dictionary definitions against context results in some absurd or weak explanations. In one of his parodies of Synge, Mulligan uses the word 'mavrone' (199). This, one is informed, is 'a variant of the Irish *mavourneen,* "my love, my darling".'[16] As in the case of 'scutter', the context suggests that the explanation is wrong. Mavrone (*mo bhrón*) means my sorrow or alas; it is not a variant of mavourneen (*mo mhuirnín*). The word 'priesteen' (215) in the same episode is explained as 'Irishism: "little priest".'[17] If the word simply means little priest, why did Joyce use the Anglo-Irish word instead of the English phrase? The English phrase is not the equivalent of the Anglo-Irish word. The phrase is neutral; the word allows Joyce to do three things simultaneously: to be pejorative, to be accurate and to pun. Priesteen is a pejorative term; it rhymes with the name of the priest, Father Dinneen, compiler and editor of the standard Irish-English dictionary, who was a small man and whose name had been mentioned twice a few pages earlier (211). The diminutive suffix *een* is not always pejorative, as in the word 'mavourneen', but it is in words such as 'priesteen' and 'maneen'. The Citizen's term of abuse, 'shoneens' (310), is feebly explained by Gifford and Seidman as Irish for 'would-be gentlemen'.[18] They fail to note that this term, which is the Irish for 'littlejohns [Bull],' is only applied to those Irish who attempt to improve their status by rejecting their own heritage and aping English ways. At the beginning of her soliloquy, Molly refers to 'that old faggot Mrs Riordan' (738). Faggot is explained as 'English slang for an old, shrivelled woman,'[19] which is correct. However, in Anglo-Irish speech it is a term of contempt for an angry female regardless of age. Mrs Riordan's performance at the Christmas dinner in *A Portrait* illustrates the accuracy of Molly's word choice and the inadequacy of the explanation. It is interesting to note that Molly uses the word exactly as Wolfe Tone used it in his diary in 1796.[20]

A hidden difficulty of the Anglo-Irish dialect for those who are unfamiliar with it is the fact that it contains a considerable number of words which are not the English words they appear to be. There is a prominent example in 'Sirens', which is again missed by Gifford and Seidman. Twice Bald Pat, the waiter, is described as being 'bothered' (*U* 267, 280), which is the Anglicized form of the Irish word for deaf. The word also appears in *Finnegans Wake* in which Joyce frequently uses this feature of the dialect.

Joyce's exploitation of the resources of the Anglo-Irish dialect is most extensive in *Finnegans Wake*. The first and most consistently exploited feature of the dialect is its distinctive pronunciations of certain common words, which are used to extend the meaning of the text. The first example is a pun in the title. Anglo-Irish speech preserves the eighteenth-century pronunciation of a large number of words containing the sound usually represented in standard English by the digraph *ea*. This is such a prominent feature of the dialect that the pronunciation of one such word, Jesus, is regarded by many as the *sine qua non* of Dublin speech. In 'Scylla and Charybdis' Mulligan accuses Stephen of ingratitude because he slated Lady Gregory's 'drivel to Jaysus' in one of his book reviews (*U* 216). Wake is a commonly heard pronunciation of weak, and is used by Joyce to hint at the condition of Finnegan, a fact which is later confirmed in an Ulster accent: 'Tam Fanagan's weak yat' (276.21–22). Campbell and Robinson state that the 'first clue to the method and the mystery of the book is found in the title,' but in their detailed explanation of the meaning of the title they seem completely unaware of this pun.[21]

The Anglo-Irish pronunciation of the short *e* vowel allows Joyce many opportunities for puns. The opportunities can best be suggested by telescoping a number of examples into one sentence: 'Thim' (215.33) 'illigant' (14.04) 'hin' (12.17) 'iggs' (12.14) would feed 'tin' (262.29) 'min' (12.03). In a work in which there is so much emphasis on rivers, 'foriver' (13.17) is an apt spelling of forever. There is a pointed reference to this feature of Anglo-Irish pronunciation in 'The Study Period': 'he's turning tin for ten' (262.29).

The English voiced and voiceless interdental fricative sound *th* does not exist in the Irish language, which accounts for the difficulty the sound causes many Irishmen. Some of the earliest representations of Anglo-Irish speech mock attemps by the Irish to cope with the sound. There are two examples in the first line of the seventeenth-century, anti-Irish song 'Lili Burlero', part of which is parodied in *Finnegans Wake* (206.04). The song begins: 'Ho! broder Teague, dost hear de decree?'[22] There are four examples in as many words in Joyce's mockery of the broadcasts of 2 R.N., the Irish Free State Radio: 'Dis and dat and dese and dose!' (528.26). This is an old taunt used by educated Irishmen to mock their less polished countrymen. In *Ulysses* Stephen imagines his father mocking his in-laws: 'De boys up in de hayloft' (38).

Joyce does not ignore the considerable regional variations in Anglo-Irish pronunciation. The accents of the four provinces can be detected in the speech of H.C.E.: 'his derry's own drawl and his corksown blather and his doubling stutter and his gullaway swank' (197.04–06). Joyce drew Harriet Shaw Weaver's attention to his use of accents from the four provinces in the work (*SL* 297). There is one topical example of his use of a provincial accent to extend the meaning of the text. By spelling that most enduring – if not most endearing – of Ulster slogans exactly as it is pronounced, 'to hull with the poop' (416.32), he adds to it new and unfamiliar geographical and nautical dimensions.

Much of the Anglo-Irish vocabulary of *Finnegans Wake* is disguised, but even undisguised Anglo-Irish words elude critics. Campbell and Robinson take 'Pattern' (festival of a patron saint, 237.13) at its face value, and paraphrase 'the bugganeering wanderducken' (323.01) as 'That buccaneering Flying Dutchman! '[23] Since 'buggan' is the Anglicized form of the Irish term *bogán*, an egg laid without a shell, the phrase should be paraphrased 'the wandering duck that

130

lays eggs without shells.' The disguise is thin in the case of words which retain the eighteenth-century pronunciation of *ea*: 'bait' (beat, 180.31); 'hate' (heat, 116.23); 'lave' (leave, 168.02); 'mate' (meat, 270, n.2); 'mainest' (meanest, 396.21); 'pace' (peace, 612.03); 'sate' (seat, 550.21); 'say' (sea, 371.32); 'stale' (steal, 9.18). The phrase 'the tay is wet' (12.16) appears to be a truism about a Scottish river, but it is the Anglo-Irish phrase for 'the tea is ready', and, as the context suggests, a euphemism for sexual intercourse.

Many words which appear to be standard English words are also Anglo-Irish dialect words: 'bothered' (deaf, 619.08); 'chiseller' (child, 482.06); 'dark' (blind, 93.27, 251.24, also *U* 181); 'lashings' (plenty, 134.02); 'lathering' (beating, 200.34); 'make' (halfpenny, 313.28); 'Rawmeash' (nonsense, 260, n.1); 'turnover' (loaf of bread, 12.16); 'yoke' (vehicle, 469.36). In every case it is clear from the context that Joyce is playing on the meaning of the word in Anglo-Irish speech. One of the washerwomen in 'Anna Livia' says to the other: 'Tell me the trent of it while I'm lathering hail out of Denis Florence MacCarthy's combies' (200.33–35). Some of these words are of Irish derivation: 'bothered' from *bodhar* (deaf); 'Rawmeash' from *ráiméis* (nonsense); and, as one might expect, this fact is noted by Joyce: 'Rawmeash, quoshe with her girlic teangue' (260, n.1).

Colcannon is an Irish dish of potatoes mashed with butter, milk, chopped cabbage and chopped scallions. Every time the dish is alluded to, the disguise of the word increases: 'hailcannon' (174.22); 'Cailcainnin' (391.33); and, finally, 'kailkannonkabbis' (456.07), when it appears in a catalogue of dishes, which includes 'boiled protestants' (potatoes, 456.03). This name for potatoes has its origin in a tendency of Protestants to combine proselytising with relief of distress in times of famine, an activity which has spawned a number of derisive terms, such as 'soupirs' (*FW* 453.12) and 'Swaddlers' (*D* 22), applied to those who converted for food or clothing. In *Ulysses* Bloom muses: 'They say they used to give pauper children soup to change to protestants in the time of the potato blight' (180). The traditional Irish hallowe'en cake, barmbrack (*bairghean breac*, speckled cake), which is mentioned in 'Clay' (*D* 110), appears as 'Saint Barmabrac's (*FW* 274.12) and later as 'Abarm's brack' (*FW* 531.10). The statement 'I awed to have scourched his Abarm's brack for him' is paraphrased by Campbell and Robinson as 'I ought to have scorched his back for him,' even though the context is studded with references to baking.[24] Some Anglo-Irish words in

Richard Wall

Finnegans Wake are so heavily disguised that one must hear them read by Joyce in order to detect them. 'Mezha' (214.07) does not look like an Anglo-Irish word, but when Joyce recorded 'Anna Livia,'[25] he pronounced it 'Wisha' (well or indeed), which is an Anglicized form of the Irish *má seadh*.[26]

Finnegans Wake is peppered with the common excremental and sexual slang terms heard in Dublin: 'diddies' (nipples, 179.18); 'Gee' (vagina, 436.08); 'Gipoo' (semen, 276.17); 'greenhouse' (public toilet, 362.34, 377.05, also in *U* 153, 252, 753); 'kip' (brothel, 243.22, also in *U* 303); 'mickey dazzlers' (prick teasers, 444.27); 'po' (chamberpot, 622.07), and 'poing' (204.12); 'pooley' (urine, 206.28); 'relic' (penis, 435.22); 'touch' (sexual intercourse, 532.22, also in *P* 229 and *U* 89). Campbell and Robinson take greenhouse at its face value,[27] but it is quite clear that Joyce means toilet: 'The groom is in the greenhouse, gattling out his. Gun!' (377.05–06). Only three of these terms, 'gee', 'gipoo' and 'greenhouse' (from the paint colour), appear to be limited to Dublin; the rest are common in many parts of the country. The history of Dublin is reflected in the fact that the list contains words of English, Scandinavian and Irish origin. Most are English, but one, 'kip', is Danish, while another, 'diddies', is Irish. The Danish for brothel is *horekippe*; the Irish for nipple is *did*. Joyce appears to have anticipated and mocked discussions such as this on the vocabulary of the work. The word 'hole' (266.02) has the following footnote: 'I have heard this word used by Martin Halpin, an old gardener from the Glens of Antrim who used to do odd jobs for my godfather, the Rev. B. B. Brophy of Swords' (266, n.2).

Anglo-Irish phrases in *Finnegans Wake* are accorded the treatment given to Anglo-Irish words. Some are undisguised, while others are very heavily disguised. An undisguised and lightly disguised phrase is 'on his keeping' (on the run, 191.11–12), which later appears as 'on whosekeeping' (422.14). In *A Portrait* Cranly calls Temple 'a go-by-the-wall' (a sneak, 201); it appears in *Finnegans Wake* as 'go-be-dee' (437.07). The extent to which some phrases are disguised is illustrated on the first page of the work. Without Joyce's assistance, it is unlikely that any reader would realize that 'rory end to the regginbrow' (04.13–14) is, among other things, the phrase 'bloody end to the lie,' which means 'no lie' (*Letters* I, 248).

The most important and pervasive Anglo-Irish phrase in the

work is one which is also used by the ranting Citizen in *Ulysses*: '*Sinn Fein! . . . Sinn fein amhain!* (Ourselves! Ourselves alone!, 306). Twice Molly makes Freudian slips when she uses the phrase: 'Sinner Fein' (748, 772). Her slips are echoed in *Finnegans Wake*: 'sinnfinners' (36.26); 'paid full feins for their sins' (330.18); and, 'the loves of sinfintins' (624.18). St Fintan and Finn can also be detected in 'sinfintins'. St Fintan built an oratory on Howth, which in Irish mythology and *Finnegans Wake* (7.28–29) is the head of the sleeping Finn. In his essays, 'Ireland, Island of Saints and Sages' and 'Fenianism', Joyce sees the Sinn Féin movement possibly leading to the long awaited resurrection of Ireland and its people (*CW* 173, 191). This view is reflected in *Finnegans Wake*, in which the movement is linked with the anticipated resurrection of Finn and H.C.E.: 'that day hwen . . . (some Finn, some Finn avant!), he skall wake from earthsleep, haught crested elmer, in his valle of briers of Greenman's Rise O, (lost leaders live! the heroes return!) and o'er dun and dale the Wulverulverlord (protect us!) his mighty horn skall roll, orland, roll' (73.36–74.05). Sinn Féin is among the cries which awaken Finn and H.C.E. at the dawn of the new era: 'Sonne feine, somme feehn avaunt! ' (593.08–09). It is even used in connection with the radio set in H.C.E.'s pub: 'Our svalves are svalves aroon! ' (311.17); and, 'Our set, our set's allohn' (324.15–16). The work suggests that the popularity of Sinn Féin is due to the fact that its battle hymn (*rosc catha*) appeals to basic human needs such as wine (*fíon*), bread (*arán*) and song (*amhrán*): 'the bouckaleens shout their roscan generally (seinn fion, seinn fion's araun.)' (42.11). John Garvin states correctly that ' "seinn fion's araun" means Sinn Féin's song, i.e., *The Soldier's Song*', but he overlooks the allusion to the economic promises of Sinn Féin in the play on the Irish words for bread and wine.[28]

Joyce's increasing use of the Anglo-Irish dialect as he matured parallels a fundamental change in his approach to his subject, which is reflected in his style. *Dubliners* and *Finnegans Wake* have certain features in common, but they were obviously conceived and written in a different spirit. The difference is that between the classical spirit and the romantic spirit, as he understood them. He said that he wrote *Dubliners* 'in accordance with what [he understood] to be the classical tradition of [his] art' (*Letters* I, 60). Some of the characteristics of the Anglo-Irish dialect are such that its extensive use in the work would have been incompatible with his attempt to write in 'a style of scrupulous meanness'. Part of his description of the romantic spirit in his first essay on Mangan could, but for its obvious hostility, serve as a partial description of the spirit in which *Finnegans Wake* was conceived and written: 'The romantic school is often and grievously misinterpreted, not more by others than by its own, for that impatient temper which, as it could see no fit abode here for its ideals, chose to behold them under insensible figures, comes to disregard certain limitations, and, because these figures are blown high and low by the mind that conceived them, comes at times to regard them as feeble shadows moving aimlessly about the light, obscuring it' (*CW* 74). In *Stephen Hero* Stephen states his conception of the term romantic: 'The heroic, the fabulous, I call romantic' (97). By these conceptions of the term, *Finnegans Wake* is romantic in spirit, and Joyce's massive use of the Anglo-Irish dialect in the work is an integral part of that spirit. The dialect allows him to escape some of the limitations of standard English and multiply the meaning of the text. The dialect also reflects the Irish ethos of the work, and helps to convey its essentially comic tone.

NOTES

1 Brendan O Hehir, *A Gaelic Lexicon for 'Finnegans Wake' and Glossary for Joyce's Other Works* (Berkeley: University of California Press, 1967); and Helmut Bonheim, *A Lexicon of the German in 'Finnegans Wake'* (Berkeley: University of California Press, 1967).
2 All references to Joyce's works are cited parenthetically in the text using the following abbreviations:

CP   *Collected Poems* (New York: Viking Press, 1957).

CW   *The Critical Writings of James Joyce,* ed. Ellsworth Mason and Richard Ellmann (New York: Viking Press, 1959).

D   *'Dubliners': Text, Criticism, and Notes,* ed. Robert Scholes and A. Walton Litz (New York: Viking Press, 1969).

E   *Exiles* (New York: Viking Press, 1951).

FW   *Finnegans Wake* (New York: Viking Press, 1959).

Letters, *Letters of James Joyce, I,* ed. Stuart Gilbert (New York:
I, II   Viking Press, 1966). Vol. II, ed. Richard Ellmann (New York: Viking Press, 1966).

P   *A Portrait of the Artist as a Young Man,* text corrected from the Dublin Holograph by Chester G. Anderson and edited by Richard Ellmann (New York. Viking Press, 1964).

SH   *Stephen Hero*, ed. John J. Slocum and Herbert Cahoon (New York: New Directions, 1963).

SL   *Selected Letters of James Joyce*, ed. Richard Ellmann London: Faber and Faber, 1975).

U   *Ulysses* (New York: Random House, 1961).

3   He called the poem 'Cabra' in 1906, 'Ruminants' in 1918 and 'Tilly' when it appeared in 1927 (*Letters* II, 181).

4   *Irish-English Dictionary*, ed. Patrick S. Dinneen (Dublin: Educational Company of Ireland, 1927), p. 1271. This dictionary is the reference for all Irish words in the paper.

5   P. W. Joyce, *English As We Speak It In Ireland* (London: Longmans, Green, 1910), p. 260.

6   *Ibid.*, p. 143-44.

7   *Ibid.*, p. 351.

8   *Musical Allusions in the Works of James Joyce* (Albany: State University of New York Press, 1974), p. 22.

9   *A Gaelic Lexicon for 'Finnegans Wake' and Glossary for Joyce's Other Works*, p. 335.

10   *The English Dialect Dictionary*, ed. Joseph Wright (Oxford: Henry Frowde, 1905), V, 562.

11   *Notes for Joyce: An Annotation of James Joyce's 'Ulysses'* (New York: Dutton, 1974), p. 182.

12   'Allusions in *Ulysses:* Random Addenda and Corrigenda for Thornton,' *James Joyce Quarterly*, 13 (Fall 1975), 54-55.

13   J. M. Synge, *Collected Works*, III, ed. Ann Saddlemyer (London: Oxford University Press, 1968), 11-13.

14   Gifford and Seidman, p. 7.

15   *A Skeleton Key to 'Finnegans Wake'* (New York: Viking Press, 1961), p. 221.

16   Gifford and Seidman, p. 183.

17   *Ibid.*, p. 205.

18   *Ibid.*, p. 277.

19   *Ibid.*, p. 498.

20   Quoted in *Hibernia Fortnightly Review*, June 13, 1975, p. 24.

21   Campbell and Robinson, p. 4.

22   Thomas Percy, *Reliques of Ancient English Poetry* (London: Henry Washbourne, 1844), II, 388.

23   Campbell and Robinson, p. 151, 207.

24   *Ibid.*, p. 320.

25   James Joyce reading from *Ulysses* and *Finnegans Wake:* Caedmon Recording TC 1340.

26   P. W. Joyce, p. 296.

27   Campbell and Robinson, p. 235.

28   'Some Irish and Anglo-Irish Allusions in *Finnegans Wake*,' *James Joyce Quarterly*, 11 (Spring 1974), 270.

DENIS DEVLIN: POET OF DISTANCE

BRIAN COFFEY

Recently, a friend of mine remarked of his new collection of verses that he was not sure what to say about them, because he was not yet at a sufficient 'distance' from them for judgement. Distance in that usage occurs frequently in the current chat-us-up of versifiers, writers, academics and critics, and need not concern us here.

The late Randall Jarrell, concluding an essay on the poetry of Robert Frost, wrote:

> To have the distance from the most awful and most nearly unbearable parts of the poems, to the most tender, subtle and loving parts, a distance so great; to have the whole range of being treated with so much humour and sadness and composure, with such plain truth; to see that a man can still include, connect and make humanly understandable or humanly un-understandable so *much* – this is one of the freshest and oldest of joys. . . .[1]

'Distance' there suggests the range of being, held – as it were, *displayed* – in its far wide sweep, in the poet's grasp; one thinks of that frenzied Shakespearian poet rolling his eye from earth to heaven, from heaven to earth: how different *that* is from the pusillanimity of the Eliotish 'human kind cannot bear much reality', in a world where, at the least, people get themselves born, procreate and die – no less, *die*. And it suggests, does that distance, that the poet at his best comprehends and manifests in his verses the immensity within which all of us are, should I say, interned. But 'distance', in that usage, applies to many poets, not least to Devlin when, for example, his seeing opposes the cold, peaceful stars to our little world – the world in which we build basilicas and sicken at the sight of two-headed calves.[2] One could, of course,

137

replace 'distance' by other equally apt terms to name the literary
quality Jarrell is referring to.

In dictionaries, we find 'distance' in the sense of the physical
gap between two individuated places. The term stands there for
something less sophisticated, less abstract, than the notion of
space. It is used in the arts, in sports, in trades, in industrial practice – wherever concrete interval of some kind is present; and, in
the way transfers of usage go, it is applied to temporal interval and
to reaches of inner experience. Because of this polyvalence of the
term, one feels almost impelled to work inductively to attempt to
see whether 'distance' might not perhaps, in some manner yet to
be exemplified, apply as much to Devlin the poet as to Devlin's
poems.

Naturally I do not mean to suggest that one wants to fling the
term like a macintosh around those poems so as to hide them in
the remote security of the taken-as-brilliant-but-unreadable master-
pieces of non-proletarian non-immediacy: not at all. I am here to
make Devlin's work better known. As for immediacy and present
vogues, let us rule them out of court at once in the representation
of the jeans-junction guitar-playing bard – I mean 'second-class
versifier' – falling around his instrument into a rodinesque pose of
extreme concentration whence, following a silence, sad and
fraught, he moans out to a hesitant one-finger accompaniment an
improvisation in, if you can call them that, words like:

Wann' out
out ride back
be no moar
not feeeex
walls to wall me
wann' out
outa meeeee

Such immediacy, infected by pretensions of sincerity, clad in the
gear of revolt from traditional craft, aspiring to the condition of a
perfectly eroded, formless uttering of unintelligibly pregnant
sound, is quite different from that mastery of the immediately
rousing political verse which was the fruit of Mayakovsky's concern over two decades with prosody, a prosody shaped to the shape
of his immense footsteps as he roamed the streets of pre-revolu-

tionary St Petersburg/Petrograd/Leningrad. In Mayakovsky's case, there lay between him and the tiny *agitprop* figures of an already ossifying bureaucracy, a great distance – that from the sublime to the ridiculous. And I mention Mayakovsky on purpose, because it is sometimes claimed nowadays that poetry should be political, and also because Mayakovsky's work was a strong influence in Devlin's development, but yet did not move Devlin towards the writing of political verse. As it turned out, Devlin's 'distance' from the political scene was necessary for his poetry.

So, to return to the claim that poets should be political; the argument goes that poets owe allegiance to life, politics is the means of changing life, and therefore poets should be political. It is further asserted that poets who declare their allegiance to language are suspect because, believe it or not, it has been said (with quasi-quotes from Wittgenstein): 'Objects can only be named; signs represent them; one can speak about them; one cannot put them into words.'[3] What a mess! Thus to use emotive words like 'allegiance', 'life'; debased words like 'politics'; misunderstood words like 'poet'; and thus to use a philosophising genius who wanted nothing better than that each he/she should think his/her thoughts in personal freedom in front of whatever happened to be the case, replacing him by the second or third generation arguers from what they suppose to be fixed wittgensteinian principles! Thank goodness we can name rocks 'rocks', understand rocks, like Guillevic write poems of rocks, and yet have the rocks well and truly at a distance. What a blessing we don't have the rocks in our heads in all their petrine rigidity!

But I shall not pursue a discussion about poetry and politics, interesting as it might be, and affording at this present time in the twentieth century such wonderful opportunity for dealing with the self-stultified. I merely confine myself to stating that, as a matter of fact, Devlin would not have had any sympathy for the 'poetry must be political' thesis. He expressed himself clearly on the matter in verses in one of his later poems, succeeding in placing both politicians and ecclesiastics at a distance from himself in the name of personal dignity; thus, from his 'The Colours of Love':

I met a kinsman in the market-place,
Singing, and as he sang my courage grew,

Brian Coffey

It was about betrayal and disgrace,
He said 'Love fails but love of love stays true'.

Singing in vain and formal in the shade
The noble poverty those houses made.

Divinities of my youth,
Expound to me my truth;

Whether from Judah or Rome
Or my nearer Gaeldom.

The driven horse formalises
His speed for prestige and for prizes,

The girl swinging on the swing
Of the convent, makes me sing

And apples drop like centuries from
The tree of life, so long in bloom;

But divinities of my youth,
You can no longer tell the truth,

It is too much a struggle to
Keep quality confined to you.[4]

Curiously enough, in an interesting book *Two Decades of Irish Writing*, Seamus Deane, writing on 'Irish Poetry and Nationalism', remarks:

> Only Denis Devlin . . . (in the period 1930–55) . . . attempts to make some reconciliation between poetry and politics in, for instance, his poem 'The Tomb of Michael Collins' – and that is a sad failure.[5]

But Deane has got it wrong: people like me who were boys in 1920 and 1921 recall mainly a great heroic presence or remember to have heard someone say of Collins: 'He is a statesman' – and that is a word we do not often use today. Just listen to the personal reverence and affection of Devlin for a man who had been in his father's house, and judge of the remove from politics, or so-called reconciliations between poetry and politics.

> Much I remember of the death of men,
> But his I most remember, most of all,
> More than the familiar and forgetful
> Ghosts who leave our memory too soon –
> Oh, what voracious fathers bore him down! . . .
>
> He was loved by women and by men,
> He fought a week of Sundays and by night
> He asked what happened and he knew what was –
> O Lord! how right that them you love die young! . . .
>
> The newsboys knew and the apple and orange women
> Where was his shifty lodging Tuesday night;
> No one betrayed him to the foreigner,
> No Protestant or Catholic broke and ran
> But murmured in their heart: here was a man!
>
> Then came that mortal day he lost and laughed at,
> He knew it as he left the armoured car,
> The sky held in its rain and kept its breath;
> Over the Liffey and the Lee, the gulls,
> They told his fortune which he knew, his death. . . .[6]

One may ask oneself what Shakespeare was alluding to when he spoke of 'art made tongue-tied by authority': but Devlin, who well knew what role Plato's ideal state would have imposed on poets, understood very well that to aim at poems – he would not have allowed that a man or woman can *decide* to, undertake to, write a poem – implies a freedom that neither reasons of state nor policing power can be permitted to restrain or constrain. Coventry Patmore expressed the poet's character when he wrote:

> The truth is great and shall prevail,
> When none cares whether it prevail or not.[7]

True, yes true: and it helps to put oneself, as Devlin did, at a remove from politics.

Brian Coffey

I have had to clear the ground a little in order to be able to present three aspects of distance connected with Devlin and his poetry. What I do have to say formed only slowly in the course of my thinking about this paper.

First then, in an account of Devlin which I wrote for *University Review*[8] (of which Professor Reynolds was then the brilliant editor), – and this was shortly after Devlin's sudden death in 1959 – I drew attention to the reserve which his student contemporaries had noticed and which others later, including the Italian novelist Silone, would recognise as part and parcel of the man. Reserve, placing a man at a distance from others, is founded, one supposes, on the freedom we humans have to give or withhold our love as regards others. Reserve will normally increase with the years as a function of developing character in conditions of increasing responsibility. It lessens as physical strength lessens, a fact which Silone noted in reflecting on the inexplicable sadness and appeal of Devlin in his final years before he succumbed to leukaemia. Such reserve suffuses a poet's work with a quality of monumental stability. The young Devlin responded to the phantasmagoria of history, its liturgy, stateliness and aura of noble causes, (only in his later years would he have accepted a pun on 'noble' and 'no bull') as the ambiguities and sarcasms of his poem 'Lough Derg' bear witness to. In his student days, he responded to the lower surrogates of reserve translating itself into contemptuous words of command. For example, he was fond of recalling a passage from Racine's *Britannicus* in which Nero, having ordered Narcisse, governor of Britannicus, to draw near, turns to his guards standing at attention to say: *'Et vous; qu'on se retire.'* The combination of the personal *vous* with the indefinite *on*, in a phrase possibly untranslatable into English, delighted Devlin who saw a source for the phrase in Racine's experience of the Versailles court where he must have heard Louis XIV, in theatrical manifestation of the kingly 'thing', place his subjects where they belonged – at a good distance from their king.

Devlin's personal reserve placed a distance between himself and others of such a kind that increasingly, as time passed, one sensed in him something of that world of realities,

    degree, priority and place,
Insisture, course, proportion, season, form,
Office and custom, in all line of order . . .[9]

142

without which, according to Shakespeare, we cannot keep the wolf from civilisation's throat. Sheltered by the powers of that moral universe, Devlin managed to protect and cultivate the capacities, fragile and always at risk, of the poet he aspired to be. He made a human, worthy distance serve his muse. And, as a result, he could see others with unbiased clarity; some of the specificity of his poetry resides in that clarity based on respect for himself and others. For example, in the following poem, written late in his life, that clarity is manifest.

MR ALLEN

From Dreghorn to the Royal and Antient Borough
Of Irvine, Mr Allen walked my road,
I waited for him while the amber bees
Danced in the window up and down the sunlight,
Old friezecoat teacher with his violin
Under his arm, which in his mind he played:

His red Scots Guard's moustaches turning white,
He played back all his life those seven miles:
His ear was antiquarian, yet he heard
All the fledglings fumbling in the hedgerows
Whose song I knew; and all ephemeras, too.

Mr Allen stamped into the schoolroom
From Tierra del Fuego, worlds away;
In vain seals barked in his unpublished concert –
It was before those mimes, the Elder Persons
Took on their tragic minatory role. . . .

II

Sad! to his numbered years the avid summer
Firing the hedgerows, sounded Omen! Omen!
But cool and sweet I had the room arranged:
Dark red chrysanthemums, the dead, the dead,
Like the flare above the steelworks of Kilwinning,
Like the ashes in the pipe which he put down,

He put the bow down, too: 'Mr Allen, Mr Allen,
If it's true we'll never play again together:

143

Brian Coffey

It's true your only heaven is in my mind!
Even your cousin ghosts by now have left you . . .
What pain, what pride, what persiflage your life!
Teaching Glasgow brats, and then for years
With bronze translated Spaniards in the pampas,
On horseback with your pipe and violin.'[10]

Let us now, secondly, return to Randall Jarrell who reviewed
Devlin's *Lough Derg and Other Poems* when that book was published in New York. Randall Jarrell was undoubtedly a perceptive
and helpful critic who frequently found the lapidary phrase to
enshrine exact intuitions; but on this occasion, writing perhaps in
that ill wind which has for so long blown over Ireland from
Majorca, he fails to do justice to his subject. His failure, however,
will help us in our discovery of Devlin's achievement. Jarrell
writes:

> Denis Devlin is plainly a writer of intelligence and informa-
> tion, and he has a gift for language – for MacNeice's language
> especially; but it does not seem to me that he has yet managed
> to make a good poem out of what he has. He does not seem to
> have enough realisation of the demands the poem makes upon
> the poet – the demands that exclude the bad, mediocre and a
> great many details from the completed work. He concentrates
> from instant to instant upon the parts, usually very rhetorical
> parts, and lets the whole take care of itself. He has a distracting
> method, persisted in for its own sake, of continually thinking
> about other people's poems or remarks, his own historical or
> cultural or geographical information, and making so many overt
> or covert allusions to all this that the reader realises he is being
> taken on an expensive, cultivated, expected series of digressions,
> a Grand Tour.[11]

Dear! dear! But there is worse to come – and I quote:

One reads:
> Come up! Up up! The thunder at one with your voices in
> order chants, things
> Are with you, rolling her rump, Earth in bacchantic rumbas
> grave swings . . .

144

and one reflects, 'with an awed contempt', that Tennyson had to write 'Locksley Hall', Auden his parody of it and MacNeice his 'Eclogue at Christmas' in order that this couplet and its miserable siblings might exist.[12]

The argument, based on an assumed immediate revulsion from the couplet quoted, is that Devlin, who is said to ape MacNeice's language, has written in 'Bacchanal' (the final title of the poem from which the couplet is taken), a third generation piece of verbal spin-off from Tennyson followed by Auden plus MacNeice. We are asked to believe that that ancestry was *necessary* in order that that 'bad, unkempt' poem, 'Bacchanal' might come to be. It doesn't say much for Jarrell's genetics that such 'excellency' should beget what is, in his view, such a botch.

Here, in parentheses, I must say that when, as students, Devlin and I considered prosody, fortified by thorough reading of Saintsbury's history of English prosody, we came jointly to the conclusion that we could analyse English verse in terms of patterns of stresses, dispensing with, for example, the notion of metrical feet. We were well aware of mild and strong stressing of syllables and of unstressed syllables in a verse. This made for differences from analyses of verse based on the older prosody descended to us from the graeco-roman world. Thus, where the traditional prosodist might point to eight feet, we might well read seven main stresses. It has been pointed out to me that all this is well known in the world of Anglo-Irish verse and its relation to the older gaelic forms: what was not then taken account of is the fact that Devlin's verse rhythms are not always based on Anglo-Irish plus latent gaelic forms.

So, using the technical language which Devlin and I used to facilitate our personal discussion about poems, we can return to Randall Jarrell's examples. 'Locksley Hall' is built on a verse of seven main stresses and the licence of as many unstressed outriding syllables as are wanted, together with occasional mildly stressed syllables; and the positioning of the main stresses is continuously varied with the enormous Tennysonian skill. It begins with the return of a man to the scene of his beginnings:

Comrades, leave me here a little, while as yet 'tis early dawn:
Leave me here, and when you want me, sound upon the bugle-
horn.

'Tis the place, and all around it, as of old the curlews call,
Dreary gleams about the moorland, flying over Locksley Hall.[13]

This man recalls an earlier springtime in which his to-be-forever-
lost beloved married another. The verse modulates into that Tennysonian self-pity beneath which one hears the hungry animal growl,
passes on to visions of the great future of togetherness when the
war drums throb no longer and the flags of battle are furled in
Man's Parliament, in a Federated World: and thence to a rejection of past love and aspirations of pure knowledge, in order to
embrace power, progress and change, down whose ringing groves
the great world will spin forever, for forward-looking, power-
intoxicated man. And before we bid farewell to this prosodic
monument from an age of vanished dreams, let us remember that
Tennyson had not heard Macmillan usher in 'the wind of change'.
So 'Locksley Hall'.

Auden's parody of that poem, to be found in the 1930 volume of
his *Poems*, (the parody has not been reprinted in any later volume
of Auden's verse: does one wonder why?), employs the same basic
seven stresses with unlimited unstressed syllables as in 'Locksley
Hall', but less the Tennysonian mastery of modulation. The parody
provides a sort of contrast between *what was* and *what will be*,
spoken antiphonally in the voices of respectively the sly, slick fifth-
former, and the disapproving, arrogant first-year sixth-former. It
begins:

Get there if you can and see the land you once were proud to
own,
Though the roads have almost vanished and th' expresses never
run.
Smokeless chimneys, damaged bridges, rotting wharves and
choked canals,
Tramlines buckled, smashed trucks lying on their side across the
rails.

Such is the setting, and here is one instance of its continuing:

Perfect pater. Marvellous mater. Knock the critic down who
dares . . .
Very well, believe it, copy, till your hair is white as theirs . . .[14]

Auden rejected the piece from his canon: where did Jarrell discover its excellence?

The MacNeice *Eclogue*, written I believe in 1933 and first published in 1935, is a dialogue between two moralists, in verses for which the norm is six stresses dropping occasionally down to four stresses, very occasionally rising above six. I give one example of the language, the magpie language, and the insufferable, moralising tone.

> In the country they are still hunting, in the heavy shires
> Greyness is on the fields and sunset like a line of pyres
> Of barbarous heroes smoulders through the ancient air
> Hazed with factory dust and, orange opposite, the moon's glare,
> Goggling yokel-stubborn through the iron trees,
> Jeers at the end of us, our bland ancestral ease;
> We shall go down like palaeolithic man
> Before some new Ice Age or Genghiz Khan.[15]

With those examples of Jarrell's evidence in memory, let us now listen to the poem from which Jarrell misused a couplet. The poem, called 'Bacchanal' in the *Intercessions* volume of 1937, and later, was composed almost in the entirety of its final form during the years 1931–3 when Devlin was in Paris; at the time, he was influenced mainly by his reading of Mayakovsky's *Cloud in Trousers*, a French version of which had just become available. Devlin knew nothing of MacNeice then. Originally, 'Bacchanal' was called 'News of Revolution', and paid tribute to those revolutionaries of all ages who achieve a view of, but do not enter, their land of promise. Based on a verse of eight stresses, with outriding partly stressed or unstressed syllables in varying number, the language of the poem displays a masterly liberty in the positioning of stresses, uses the image very often surrealistically, employs sarcasm rather than the moralistic whinge, and achieves extraordinary vigour of rhythm quite beyond any verse ever made by MacNeice. This is how the poem begins:

> Forerunners, with knees flashing like scissors, raced by the hostile telegraph wires,
> Start for the ships with the news, Cut Through, all is against them despair inspires:

147

Brian Coffey

The poor made limp by want of cackling, brainstopped youth, a
seaweed crowd . . .
How the road that smokes through the mountains, whose
panther-bounding shadows applaud, is loud
With the confident feet of pursuing criers! their eyes diamond
with thousands of years
Of domination and lands held of fictitious papers by right of
fears
Easy on which to maintain the sneering feet of the lovely lords
of might,
They and the courtiers of prudence insured against danger of
life and number and light. . . .

And continues:

Already immense shoulders heave edgeways through heavy bales
of sleep.
Force of confederate, free flangewheels, O runners through
breakage! give them the slip:
Those with hands like shrinking linen that deprecate the state
of affairs,
Parsing attitudes, fleas in intricate corridors of interlocking
hairs,
Those that are Not So Sure that the Poor in Pogrom will not
be Rather a Bore,
Lips bitter-sweet, they Know by Culture, they know Human
Nature can Grow no More;
Those that are Game to Grin and Bear it, those that the Wear
and Tear of, that hesitate
Wagging advice faded and steaming as old maids' clothes before
the grate,
Those that My Country, that Let us Pray, that Drop by the
Way, those that are Late . . .
Oh, when damned by the sentence of guns advancing like ants
in tragic line
And stowed away in Death, their own hungry mirror, it will
be fine! . . .

And ends:

148

Joy Joy an unbetweened chorus crowds the air with sound
Burgeoning, they feel surging more loud the birth of well-being
all around
While curveting aeroplanes, leaflets released, toss through the
matador swords of the sun
And the ships cheered by the seminal hail of the captain, by
the people won,
Draw white clothes on, make sure of the sea, open tanned arms
with love and take
To the long white heather of the waves, a wind of towns in cry
in wake.

Forerunners with eyes of dangerous landscapes silent among the
cheering sigh
At the flocks of aeroplanes grazing at stall across the spring
prairies of the sky.[16]

I leave it with you. On the evidence, Jarrell is, I believe, guilty of
great misjudgement. This one might excuse, perhaps, by saying
that, used as he was to the basic iambics of the English tradition,
he had failed to recognise the prosodic mastery of one whose ear
had been formed on the rhythms of a large number of languages,
and whose syntax had been constructed to hold a subject-matter
at the distance necessary for reflective empathy. The language
makes the distance, with Devlin, in even the early poems dating
from 1932, for example in the tender and reflective 'Liffey Bridge':

LIFFEY BRIDGE

Parade parade
The evening puts on
Her breath-stained jewels
Her shadowy past.

Trailing behind
Tired poses
How they all
Fulfill their station!
The young with masks and
The old with faces

149

Brian Coffey

    Such an assassin
    Such a world!

    From the bridge they admire
    Their foolish reflection
    Drowning in birth,
    Man's face and centuries
    In rivers with stars
    Fugitive wheatfields
    Giving no harvest . . .
    Here's poulticed peace.
    If dreaming of death
    Unheavened could but rend them
    With anger or envy!

    The pigeons creak
    On rusty hinges
    Turn to the window
    Bright with oranges
    And girls the girls
    The gashed fruit
    Of their mouths and smiles
    Cute as the rims
    Of their cock-eyed hats:

    In limp doorways
    They try out their heaven
    They grind at love
    With gritted kisses
    Then eyes re-opened
    Behold slack flesh
    Such an assassin
    Such a world!

    Same with all the
    Young and hopeful
    Any relief will
    Do for a spell
    Then timid masks
    Live into faces

Then there is quiet
Desperation

The houses lean
Against the wind
Won't you give over?
Say, what about
That second coming?

Deaf quay walls.
Water wears
The stone away
And out of the river
The arc-lamp rays and the
Wind weave
Try to weave
Something or other
From flight and water.[17]

Finally, we come to the central element of Devlin's poetic activity, namely his aim and search for what is most distant, most different and most distinct from us humans, and his attempt to bring that most distant beyond all sensible or imagined horizons into human proximity – close to. Michael Smith, whose New Writers' Press and review *The Lace Curtain* have served poetry and poets in Ireland so well during the last decade, has drawn attention to this aspect of Devlin's work. He writes:

Denis Devlin, having absorbed an incredible range of European influences both of the past and the present, set himself the task of exploring the possibilities of spiritual and religious salvation in the modern world. What is generally overlooked in Devlin's work is the degree to which it is socially concerned. There is, for example, a strong satirical motivation at work in many of the poems, but never explicit. Although he repudiated the aims of the British 1930's, Devlin shared something with them. The difference, drawing him closer to Eliot and away from the early Auden, lies in the religious nature of his perspectives.[18]

151

I do not feel one should go further and call Devlin a religious poet because, in these interesting times of variegated confusion, dissension and dissent – times indeed ready for Roland Knox's lethal *Creed for All* – it has become difficult to use the label of religious poet in any unambiguous sense. One has only to think of the kind of anthology of religious verse which includes at once Robinson Jeffers's 'Hooded Night', Swinburne's 'Hertha', Thompson's 'Hound of Heaven' and Timon of Athens's 'That nature, being sick of man's unkindness.' But we can follow the development of a religious theme through the entire span of Devlin's poetry.

Leaving aside the as-yet-unpublished religious verse of his schooldays – verse which reflects the habitual thoughts of a serious and pious boy – the poems most obviously concerned with religious thoughts and attitudes can be placed in a group of three poems which display a progress and a deepening of religious understanding, namely the 'Est Prodest' of 1933, the 'Lough Derg' of 1946 and 'The Passion of Christ' of 1958. Apart from these poems, there stands alone the poem called 'The Heavenly Foreigner' which we know, from the evidence of the manuscript, to have preoccupied Devlin from very early in the thirties until its publication in 1950 – following which event, Devlin continued to work over the text until his death in 1959.

'The Heavenly Foreigner' enverbs the struggle of a person who is both lover and poet with very different loves and the beloved subjects of these loves, in each of whom he sights a paradise, and for each of whom he suffers agonies of sensibility. He undergoes, often in painful and sorrowful circumstances, the labour of an independent grasping at the source of his being, a striving which is not dependent on a principle of private judgement, but is a learning the lesson of pain without the telling of lies to self – while the poet despairs of a physical body weakening towards death. Hear how this protagonist apprehends his *now*:

> The years weave through me and young men spend their time,
> Evenings of unhappiness, a great weak iris . . .
> Time does not stretch ahead of me
> As if I might unroll my scroll on it
> But it is volumed round me, thick with echoes, things
> I cannot see throughout.
> Such things so and so many years ago:

The already is my present unresolved.
Separate and self-absorbed, the friends growing older,
Return from the central mystery in the maze
To the primitive blaze of the virgin at the door;
And the mistresses of dead politicos, by the shining lakeside,
Fade, like the hatred in which their Chief went down;
So life both flares and fades in me without her –
Or no, not quite; when I think of a white
Dress along the battlements above the star-broken sea,
Or white lips in the dark stair-well, life without her
Is reading the table of contents without the book.[19]

I cannot, and in any case would not attempt to, offer a condensation of a poem every verse of whose 386 verses holds its form; but one point, I feel, should be made. Devlin had a great love for the verses of John of the Cross: nevertheless it would be a mistake, I believe, to see or try to see in 'The Heavenly Foreigner' a report of mystical experience. John of the Cross's lyrics represent his own experiences, among which some devoid of sensory or imaginary impressions; experiences of which the majority of his readers can not have had even a remote conception: 'Human knowledge,' he says, 'is not sufficient to comprehend it nor human experience to describe it, because only he who has passed through it will be able to feel it, but not to tell it.' And he recorded the fact thus: 'I entered I knew not where and remained not knowing, passing beyond all knowledge.'[20]

What is here pointed to, and named 'it', is the element of incursion, whence, into the personal within in which as patient the soul undergoes the delight of the beloved's free gift of presence of which there will be no possible report to home base. Devlin's poem remains, I judge, in the antechamber of conflicting loves and in the end resolves into something like that curiosity which Leon Bloy said consumed him at the approach of death.

Briefly now of the group of three poems referred to earlier: 'Est Prodest', first composed in 1931–3 and existing now in a number of differing versions including the final one published by Devlin in 1946, is not, on the evidence of the texts, in a satisfactory final state. The poem begins from abstract considerations to close in desires expressed for communion with a 'one' beneath a tender sky. Here is a passage from the abstract beginning:

If One, they all say,
Shows himself in us
Groups of men and women
Mnemonic said of Eden
That stink high in our nostrils
Rich and poor and dead:
Then how darkly he
Is broken among us
In frosty slopes at hazard,
Sunlight on the frangent
Mirrors of the sea.

Phrases twisted through other
Reasons reasons disproofs
Identity obscured
Like mirrors shining through other
Reasons reasons disproofs.[21]

The well-known 'Lough Derg', which excited much attention when it was published in the United States, starts from a setting on the remote islands of penance and prayer in Lough Derg visited by sinners from very early times, over one thousand years ago, and since then continuously until the present day. The poet is led to contemplate and reflect on the quality of worship during that long time while he watches the penitants making their painful bare-footed rounds of the islands. And the poet, almost a man of our own times in the situation of a Job facing – with less than Job's faith – the silence of heaven, of no whirlwind, prays finally to himself:

All indiscriminate, man, stone, animal
Are woken up in the nightmare. What John the Blind
From Patmos saw works and we speak it. Not all
The men of God nor the priests of mankind
Can mend or explain the good and broke, not one
Generous with love prove communion.[22]

Are we not, there, very close to what makes the hair stand on end, the blood run cold, extinguishing almost the soul?

Last of all, 'The Passion of Christ', noted by Silone as the poem on which Devlin spent all his efforts while his strength grew less, is the justification of the long search. Without withholdings, he has accepted whom he once called 'the pleasant Lord ascending the green slopes of the morning wind, hand held out, not a breath behind.' And what has come from the search? He has not sought the Father through the Son; rather he has sighted the Son Incarnate as the friendly man of welcomings on the Jerusalem road. At home as he has become with his Christ, he has shown us Christ as one with whom we too can be at home because of the common sharing of suffering in daily life. Devlin hardly involved himself in the small miseries of theology; one might put the position in the following way: Thomas could name the being his fingers had touched and explored as his Lord and God. Devlin I do not see putting his finger into a soldier's wounded side and *by identity* naming that soldier his Lord and God; yet the fingers Christlike would have soothed the wounded person as another Christ to be consoled. For Devlin, the mystery of the mystical body does not veil from us the void of absolute monism. Truly, as Aquinas puts it, *'Est bonatis una omnium: et multae bonitates'*. Devlin's verses at last express the infinity between us and the Godhead overcome in the Christ he brings so near, so close at hand. Or so, it seems to me, the following extracts from 'The Passion of Christ' declare:

BEFORE PILATE

To flagellate, to crown with thorns, to make
A show of man who would Man create –
Nothing much when Justice is at stake –
The conflict of laws idly becomes Fate.

The scene's complete! the filthy, wine-lit bands
Forgive Barabbas who shed blood,
Pilate, the surgeon, cleans his distant hands,
In sage disgust, praises the Good.

WAY OF THE CROSS

At every stage along that station,
Averted eyes, reluctant heart!
Mob hatred, Pharisees' elation –
His knees watery from the start,

One, Simon, in excess of passion,
Trusted his unreflecting hands;
What is this genius of compassion
That comprehends, nor understands! ...

ASCENSION

It happens through the blond window, the trees
With diverse leaves divide the light, light birds;
Aengus, the God of Love, my shoulders brushed
With birds, you could say lark or thrush or thieves

And not be right yet – or ever right –
For it was God's Son foreign to our moor:
When I looked out the window, all was white,
And what's beloved in the heart was sure,

With such certainty ascended He,
The Son of Man who deigned Himself to be:
Then when we lifted out of sleep, there was
Life with its dark, and love above the laws.[23]

NOTES

1 Randell Jarrell, *Poetry and the Age* (London, 1973 edition), pp. 69-70.
2 See Denis Devlin, *The Heavenly Foreigner* (Dublin, 1967), verses 212-5.
3 Tomas MacSheoin, *The Tablet,* Spring 1976.
4 Denis Devlin, *Collected Poems,* ed. Brian Coffey (Dublin, 1964) (hereafter referred to as *C.P.*), p. 20.
5 *Two Decades of Irish Writing* (Cheadle, Carcanet Press, 1975), p. 11.
6 *C.P.*, pp. 7-8.
7 Coventry Patmore, *The Unknown Eros,* I, xii, 9-10.
8 *University Review,* Special Denis Devlin issue, 1963.
9 Shakespeare, *Troilus and Cressida,* I, iii, 86-8.
10 *C.P.*, pp. 7-8.
11 Jarrell, op. cit., pp. 200-202.
12 *Ibid.*
13 Tennyson, *Works,* (London, 1907-08), II, 34.
14 W. H. Auden, *Poems* (1930), pp. 66, 68.

15 Louis MacNeice, *Collected Poems* (London, 1966), p. 34.
16 *C.P.*, pp. 60-4.
17 *C.P.*, pp. 95-7.
18 *Two Decades of Irish Writing*, p. 160.
19 *C.P.*, pp. 28-9.
20 *St. John of the Cross*, ed. G. Brenan (London, 1975), pp. 110, 178.
21 *C.P.*, pp. 46-7.
22 *C.P.*, p. 37.
23 *C.P.*, p. 12 and pp. 14-15.

Poems by Denis Devlin quoted in this article are reprinted by permission of the Dolmen Press, Dublin, publishers of *The Collected Poems of Denis Devlin*.

IRISH LANDSCAPE IN THE VICTORIAN THEATRE

MICHAEL R. BOOTH

The place and use of landscape in nineteenth-century theatrical art is an important and interesting one, and before going on to any consideration of the treatment of Irish landscape in this art it would be useful to say something generally about landscape and the theatre.

As we know, there was little attempt in the eighteenth-century theatre at naturalistic reproduction of the exterior or interior scene. Sets of wings, shutters, and borders were harmoniously unified in formal and stylized perspective, conveying a pictorial abstraction of nature and architecture. It was not the purpose of the scene-painter, stage carpenter, or machinist to draw the audience's attention to the background of the dramatic action, nor, technologically speaking, given the limited illuminating powers of candles and oil floats, was it possible to bathe the scene in a full flood of revealing and concentrating light. The audience, too, though intimately involved with actors performing on a large forestage to pit and side boxes in close proximity, was nevertheless separated from the scenery by the size of the forestage (considerable in the larger theatres), the necessity of placing behind the proscenium arch the grooves in which the wings and shutters changed, and the desirability of directing the principal sources of light to the illumination of actors in front of the proscenium rather than to the scenes behind them.

The romantic revolution, which affected the theatre as much as it did poetry, music, painting, and the novel, brought to the performance of drama a new aesthetic which was to dominate the stage until at least the First War. This was the pictorial aesthetic. One of the most important things about theatre in the nineteenth century was that scenic artists, managers, and audiences saw it as essentially pictorial. To illustrate a text as if by

159

pictures in a book became a primary function of stage art, and all the considerable technical resources of the theatre were bent to this purpose. From De Loutherbourg's scenery for *The Wonders of Derbyshire* at Drury Lane in 1779 to David Belasco's *Merchant of Venice* in New York in 1922, the visual realization of poetic beauty was a vital principle of production. The job of the nineteenth-century actor was seen as the poetic illustration of the text through a combination of voice, gesture, and attitude; the plasticity and mobility of his body being, by the aesthetic expression of the physical and mental techniques at his command, a continuously visual and consciously beautiful commentary on, or rather actualization of, the beauty and power of a dramatic text. Scenic illustration was a part of the same general purpose, except that on the late Victorian stage the extreme development of the pictorial aesthetic too often buried the actor and the text beneath a ponderous mass of gorgeous spectacle and archaeological realism. It was the late Victorian theatre, however, that completed the movement towards looking at a performance as if it were a picture, by the architectural invention of the 'picture-frame' stage, in which a simulated picture frame was carved and painted around a proscenium opening that also marked the front of the stage itself. Technical innovations in gaslight, limelight, and electric light meant that any depth of stage behind the proscenium arch could be brightly illuminated and scenic detail emphasized if required. Dramatic action, therefore, no longer took place before a generalized scenic background, but occurred within a detailed scenic environment. The stage was in effect a painting that moved, and the theatrical art of the time must to a significant extent be thought of as a painter's and illustrator's art.

In terms of the treatment of landscape, these were notable developments. Also notable was the fact that a remarkable number of nineteenth-century scene painters became artists of stature, such as David Cox, David Roberts, Clarkson Stanfield, and William Beverley. In the Victorian period the art of the stage and the art of the studio were closely related. Not only were artists like Ford Madox Brown, Alma-Tadema, and Burne-Jones asked to design sets and costumes for Henry Irving and Beerbohm Tree, but there is also no doubt that just as theatre practitioners approached scenic art from a painter's point of view, so painters themselves saw their paintings as theatre; John Martin and

W. P. Frith come immediately to mind. A common stage technique, in fact, was the 'realization' of a famous painting in a pictorial tableau in which the figures of actors are positioned in relation to a scenic composition in order to reproduce, three-dimensionally, a popular painting. Works by David Wilkie and Frith were 'realized' in this way, and there are many other examples.

The landscape movement in scenic art was entirely romantic in origin. De Loutherbourg himself was much influenced by Salvator Rosa, and it is interesting to see how the southern romanticism of Rosa is transformed into a British landscape of softer lights, rolling mists, and a romantic wildness sometimes verging on charm rather than expressing rugged grandeur. The gauze, the transparency, the coloured silks masking side lighting, and the diorama were all techniques appropriate to the depiction of romantic landscape on the stage. The first extensive use of such techniques was in pantomime, and since pantomime always retained a strong element of fairyland fantasy, it contrived to make the utmost imaginative demands upon the scene-painter. The second area of drama in which the romantic landscape was fundamentally important was melodrama, and here, much more than in pantomime, the scenic background could be a vital aspect of dramatic content.

The Gothic melodrama, popular from about 1790 to 1830 and much longer than that in working-class theatres, possessed a dramatic content that could obviously and appropriately be illustrated by romantic landscape. Since the Gothic melodrama dealt regularly with brigands, exiled princes, tyrants, ghosts, virtuous cottagers, unknown females and fleeing heroines, the landscape becomes central in a thematic rather than a merely decorative way. The dramatist's common purpose was to arouse fear and horror; the graveyard, the ruined abbey, the forbidding castle, the dungeon, the dark forest, and the barren moor are scenic means to this end. The hero of William Dimond's *The Foundling of the Forest* (1809) is hunted by assassins in *'another part of the forest more entangled and intricate – the tempest becomes violent – alternate lightning and utter darkness.'* One scene of C. E. Walker's *The Warlock of the Glen* (1820) depicts *'the moor by midnight. In the background are the ruins of an abbey surrounded by a few withered trees – the wind is heard at intervals, and the thunder as*

161

dying away in the distance. Stage dark.' The second scene of Charles Maturin's *Bertram* (1816) is intensely romantic in a compositional sense, but still intended to evoke apprehension and fear: *'The rocks. The sea. A storm. The convent illuminated in the background. The bell tolls at intervals. A group of* MONKS *on the rocks with torches. A vessel in distress in the offing.'* In Thomas Holcroft's *A Tale of Mystery* (1802), the villain flees through a landscape which is the very terrestrial emblem of his fear, a *'wild mountainous country . . . with pines and massy rocks. A rude wooden bridge on a small height thrown from rock to rock; a rugged mill stream a little in the background. . . . The increasing storm of lightning, thunder, hail, and rain, becomes terrible. Suitable music. Enter* ROMALDI *from the rocks, disguised like a peasant, with terror, pursued, as it were, by heaven and earth.'*

It must not be thought that melodramatic landscape exclusively emphasized the rugged, the wild, and the fearsome. Pastoral and domestic landscapes, portrayed with the same charm and poetic beauty that they displayed in contemporary watercolour painting, were common, especially in plays with village settings, or those in which harvesting and milling played a picturesque role. As the century advanced, the scene-painter's landscapes became more elaborate and detailed as the pictorial aesthetic reached full development. Perhaps one example will suffice, the scene of Dartmoor and Dartmoor prison from Watts Phillips' *Not Guilty* (1869):

> *In extreme distances a vast extent of moor, wild and undulating, with huge boulder rocks on tors. On the summit of this heap of rocks, stunted trees with other varieties of wild, coarse vegetation. Framed, so to speak, by this foreground, the quarries stretch out behind, full of coves and crevices, towering up or descending suddenly into deep fissures, old or neglected workings half-hidden by the hardy herbage which clings even to these rugged rocks. The prison is on a height: a gloomy range of buildings which, though distant, dominates by its very presence the savage scene. Convicts are grouped everywhere about at work, quarrying or wheeling off slate in red trucks, under the guard of warders.*

Such pictorial realism was unknown in the landscape scenery

of early melodramas, but the scenic reproduction of reality was a necessary part of an age whose visual taste, notably stimulated by the invention of photography, demanded a realistic – or at least a verisimilar – image of life on stage. All the same, these representations of reality had to be conveyed pictorially, and in the case of dramatic landscape they were conveyed poetically as well. This style reached its apogee in Irving's scenic compositions for the Lyceum in the 1880s and 1890s, where the visual realization of poetic beauty could be regarded as great art as well as great theatre.

The idea of the Irish landscape on the Victorian stage fitted perfectly into the theatre's larger concept of romantic realism and its implementation of the pictorial aesthetic. Well before the Victorian period, the Irish landscape possessed a strong romantic and pictorial interest for writers, artists, and the educated public. Poetry and sentimental ballads constituted one aspect of this interest, illustrated books another. The sensitive and up-to-date landscape romantic found that he could respond to the West and South of Ireland with the same feeling of the sublime and the picturesque awoken in him by North Wales, the Lake district, the Derbyshire Peaks, and the Scottish Highlands. The development of the steel engraving and the vogue for travel pictures, disseminated in annuals and other works, led to a flood of handsomely illustrated travel books in the 1830s and 1840s; for the first time the interested reader could, from a variety of publications, gain a visual impression of Irish scenery without leaving his fireside. In 1837 and 1838, for example, the volumes of *Heath's Picturesque Annual* included Irish landscapes by Thomas Creswick. Creswick himself was only one of numerous watercolour artists to make sketching and painting tours of Ireland in the first half of the century. Drawings by these artists appeared not only in annuals, but also in such works as *Ireland Illustrated* (1831), *The Scenery and Antiquities of Ireland* (1842), and *Ireland: Its Scenery, Character, etc.* (1841–43), all of them profusely illustrated. *Ireland Illustrated* tells its readers that the artists contributing to that volume were responsible for 'a great variety of subjects, all of which were picturesque and sublime.'[1] These two adjectives distinguish the treatment of Irish scenery not only in books of this kind, but also on the stage.

Irish scenes appeared frequently in pantomime, sometimes in

pieces that had nothing to do with Ireland. It was common practice for the harlequinades of early Victorian pantomimes to be interrupted by scenes – usually unrolling on a diorama – illustrative of natural beauty or man-made wonders quite irrelevant to the adventures of Harlequin, Pantaloon, and Clown. For instance, Columbine in the Adelphi pantomime for 1839, *Harlequin and Mother Red Cap,* expresses a particular desire to know something of Ireland; to satisfy her, the harlequinade comes to a stop while several scenes by William Telbin, one of the greatest Victorian scene-painters, pass in review, collectively entitled in the printed libretto 'The Beauties of Ireland, the Gem of the Sea.' *Harlequin in Ireland, Harlequin Paddy Carey and the Fairies of the Silver Forest,* and *Harlequin O'Donoghue, or The Fairy White Horse of Killarney* all introduced Irish scenic material. O'Donoghue himself was the subject of at least seven different pantomimes. Nelson Lee's *Harlequin and O'Donoghue,* an equestrian pantomime written for Astley's in 1850, introduces topical temperance themes as well as the inevitable views of Killarney. The chief evil spirit, Poteen, symbolically as well as actually drowns in the pure waters of the Lake.

The most extensive use of Irish scenery did not occur in pantomime, however, but in melodrama and romantic drama. Playwrights and scene-painters gave full theatrical expression to the general tendency to think of all Irish scenery in terms of the sublime and the picturesque. Considerably before Dion Boucicault began to write dramas with Irish settings in the 1860s, this tendency combined with a relatively new approach to Irish stage character which itself was essentially a transference of the concept of the picturesque from nature to humanity. The theoretical basis for such a concept is outlined, somewhat rhapsodically, in the introduction to *The Scenery and Antiquities of Ireland:*

We imagine we can trace in the chequered character of the Irish people a reflection of the varied aspect of the country. Their exuberant gaiety, their deep sadness, their warm affections, their fierce resentment, their smiles and tears, their love and hatred, all remind us forcibly of the lights and shadows of their landscapes; where frowning precipices and quiet glens, wild torrents and tranquil streams, lakes and woods, vales and mountains, sea and shore, are all blended by the hand of

Nature beneath a sky now smiling in sunshine, now saddening in tears.[2]

The Irish stage peasantry were presented as the equivalent of the banditti of Gothic melodrama, with a great deal, as it were, of highly selective and sensationalized early *verismo*. Appropriately picturesque in dress and appearance, they were related in composed stage groupings to what was understood as their natural habitat. In the same plays the traditional stage Irishman provided light relief, but as a comic figure he flourished primarily in comedy and farce, either in his own national environment or more often transplanted to English soil. The picturesque peasant was not a character like this at all, and had very little humour in his makeup. He fulfilled, with his fellows, in whose company he was usually seen, the role of a chorus – as important to the eye as to the ear – harmoniously linking a view of the landscape with a view of character, the whole loosely integrated in a concept of Ireland and Irish life remarkably consistent in a large number of unremarked and unremarkable plays.

Examples of this concept could be enumerated at length, but possibly reference to two or three plays would be sufficient. *Suil Dhuv the Coiner*, by Thomas Dibdin, a two-act melodrama performed at Covent Garden in 1833, is typical. The very first scene is '*a picturesque Irish cottage. A vast extent of mountain scenery in the distance;*' the curtain goes up on the heroine singing 'My Island Home.' The third scene is '*a wild landscape – sunset – a group of Irish labourers cross the hills, as returning home.*' They also sing, about Ireland and about themselves as 'children of labour.' Scene four is set in a '*dreary pass among the hills – a rude and ruined bridge, where the road divides, is a rustic inn, covering much ground, but low and thatched – a withered branch hangs over a sign protruding from the doorway.*' The weather is in keeping: '*Wind and rain heard – low thunder and distant lightning, to a few bars of characteristic music.*' The fourth scene of Act II is '*a sombre landscape – a romantic stile. The white chimney tops of* O'BYRNE'*s house seen over the foliage . . . flashes of distant lightning. A little chapel is seen in the distance.*' The final scene, an excellent specimen of romantic scene-painting, delineates an illustrator's view of Ireland as well as current ideas of contemporary art: '*A Druidical circle of rude stones.*

*Lowering, low horizon all round, with flickering lightning break-
ing through the clouds at intervals. A heavy, red, full moon, but
only half seen, rising slowly and occasionally obscured.'* Such
scenes are eminently expressive of artistic notions of the sublime
and the picturesque as applied to Ireland. In the case of this play
and many like it, the settings and scene-painting are intended to
arouse feelings of anxiety and dread – as in Gothic melodramas –
as well as romantic beauty, these feelings arising from 'the
singular wildness and peculiar character of the Irish Landscape,'[3]
as the author of the topographical descriptions in *Ireland Illustrated* puts it.

If wildness was the essential character of this landscape for the
scene-painter, the dramatist sought to embody it in the people
who populated and decorated the painter's composition. The
costume note for *Suil Dhuv the Coiner* clothes the coiner's gang
'in various peasant garbs of poverty and ferocity.' They are, the
stage directions tell us, *'dark'* and *'ill-looking'* and being desperate
criminals, they behave fittingly. The criminality of the Irish
peasantry was a feature of the nineteenth-century stage image of
Ireland, and contributed to that aspect of terror which was so
important a characteristic of the melodramatic sublime. The
eponymous peasants of H. P. Grattan's *The White Boys,* a
Lyceum drama of 1836, armed with pikes, rifles, pistols, and
knives, battle the English soldiery in a *'mountainous and rocky
pass'* by moonlight; the hero exclaims 'How can this wild work
end but in ruin and defeat? No one to control – no one to
advise – nothing but their own mad wills to lead them.' Similarly
the peasantry of Colin Hazlewood's *Poul a Dhoil,* or *The Fairy
Man,* an East End melodrama of 1865, are involved in member-
ship of a villainous secret society, the Barrymount Boys. The
scenery is picturesque: a fairground, a glen, the ruins of an
abbey, a vault under the ruins, the interior of a lead mine, and
the Devil's Pool itself. As in *The White Boys* the peasants attack
the soldiers. Politics are never very clear on the melodramatic
stage, but in many plays with Irish settings, loyalty or treason to
the crown comprises such a large part of the thematic material
that the criminality or heroism of vaguely political activity becomes a part of the supposed wildness and colour of Irish life,
and thus in turn of the romantic and the picturesque.

The leading writer of Irish plays among the Victorians, Dion

166

Boucicault, continued in the romantic and picturesque tradition but made significant adjustments in the relationship between landscape and character. *The Colleen Bawn* (1860), *Arrah-na-Pogue* (1864), and *The Shaughraun* (1874) are thoroughgoing melodramas with many of the familiar characteristics of this kind of Irish drama, but even Boucicault's landscapes are different from those in the plays we have been discussing. For one thing, there is no aspect of the sublime in his settings; that is, no landscape designed to arouse terror, fear, or even a powerful apprehension in his audiences. There is no sense in Boucicault's specific use of the Lakes of Killarney in *The Colleen Bawn,* Wicklow in *Arrah-na-Pogue,* or the Sligo coast in *The Shaughraun* of wildness, vastness, desolation, or empty barrenness. While localized, colourful, and strongly romantic, these landscapes do not partake of the pictorial ruggedness of the previous theatrical generation; they are aesthetically gentler and pleasanter, a perfect complement to the less strenuous romanticism of their inhabitants. While there may be exceptions, such as the particularly nasty peasant group in *The Shaughraun* which assists the villain – clothed, we are told, in 'various garbs of poverty and ferocity,' exactly like the coiner's gang of forty years before – Boucicault does not use the Irish peasantry as a collective embodiment of the sublime in choral form. They may act together, they may be picturesque, and they may be vicious (as when they drive the informer Harvey Duff over the cliff in *Arrah-na-Pogue*), but they are not an uncouth and savage tribe involved in continuous fighting and lesser criminal activity. The Boucicault peasant, rogue, or vagabond is not a member of a uniform group without a personality of his own, but rather an individualized and humanized being with a distinct dramatic identity. The most notable examples of this really new development are those comic men-cum-heroes played originally by Boucicault himself: Myles-na-Coppaleen, Shaun the Post, and Conn the Shaughraun. Sentimentally idealized these characters are, but romantically sublime they are not. They seem to grow naturally out of the landscape of which they are a part, for there is still in Boucicault a dramatic unity between man and nature, albeit a different sort of unity from that of his predecessors in the Irish genre.

The natural landscape of Boucicault's Irish plays is worth a brief examination which will indicate that difference, one in degree rather than kind, for his plays are also set in the Irish countryside. The first and most influential, *The Colleen Bawn,* was based upon a novel by Gerald Griffin, *The Collegians,* set around Limerick and in Killarney. Boucicault kept the locale of the play to Killarney, and we are told by Townsend Walsh, his first biographer, that he was inspired to do so by a set of steel engravings of Killarney purchased at a bookstall. The story is not authenticated, but even if it was true the illustrations only provided the initial impetus. Boucicault knew perfectly well that the 'concentrated beauties of Killarney,' in the words of *Ireland Illustrated,* would offer a suitably romantic and picturesque background for his dramatic material. And Boucicault decorates his play with this background in a way that would have met the full approval of a generation of illustrators. The author of *Ireland Illustrated* tells us of the view of the Upper Lake of Killarney: 'the nobler gratification is afforded of beholding, at a glance, one of the sublimest combinations of the delicate and the awful in the works of nature, which this singularly romantic country exhibits.'⁴ The first scene of *The Colleen Bawn* is Mrs. Cregan's house on the banks of Killarney, with Muckross Head in the background, from which shines Eily O'Connor's signal to Hardress. The second is the Gap of Dunloe at dawn, and the last scene of Act II the famous cove in which Eily is saved from drowning in the gauze waters (real water in the Princess's revival of 1896) by Myles. This was a famous scene on the stage and on sheet music covers alike, famous for its intense melodrama and striking sensational effect, but also splendidly decorative in the illustrator's sense: the dark foreground of the cave, the rock, the water, the background opening to the lake, the moonlight, Eily's red cloak and white dress. Boucicault's thorough understanding of the dramatic uses of the picturesque and its relationship to the lives of his characters is evident not only from this scene in particular, but also from the individual use of the pictorial aesthetic in his Irish plays in general.

Boucicault's other two popular Irish plays, *Arrah-na-Pogue* and *The Shaughraun,* follow a similar pattern of pictorial romanticism, although neither contains an external scene as dramatically picturesque as the cave scene in *The Colleen Bawn.* The opening scene of *Arrah-na-Pogue* reads '*Glendalough. Moonlight. The Ruins of St. Kevin's Abbey, the Round Tower, the Ruined*

Cemetery, the Lake and Mountains beyond.' As must now be clear, Boucicault was extremely fond of nocturnal and moonlight exteriors. Four important scenes in *The Colleen Bawn* occur at night; three of them are lit by the moon. There are four night exteriors in *Arrah-na-Pogue*, five in *The Shaughraun*, and moonlight shines on most of them. Sunset and dawn are other popular times of the day. The moonlight, the ruined abbey, the lake, and the mountains of the first scene of *Arrah-na-Pogue* make up a landscape very like that in Act II of *The Shaughraun*, in the scene where Conn pretends to be Robert Ffolliott in order to draw the villains' fire and ensure the hero's escape. Here are the sea, distant cliffs, a ruined abbey, and, of course, the moon, which at the end of the scene is actively dramatic rather than passively picturesque: Moya has thrown herself despairingly on Conn's body, and *'a ray of moonlight striking through the ruined window falls on the figure of the saint on the shrine, whose extended arms seem to invoke protection over the prostrate group.'* This integration of scenic beauty with dramatic effect is characteristic of Boucicault, but not of his predecessors. Yet although his use of ruined abbeys, moonlight, water, and mountains was melodramatic as well as picturesque in intention, scenic arrangements like this are discoverable in a dozen earlier books illustrative of the Irish landscape. The first scene of *The Shaughraun* could have been found in a hundred sketchbooks and finished watercolours: a humble cottage and milkmaid bent over her churn in the foreground, and behind *'the ruins of Suil-a more Castle cover a bold headland in the half distance. The Atlantic bounds the picture. Sunset.'*

An adherence to the romantic and picturesque in visual art and scene-painting usually meant a devotion to the natural landscape. However, since in much illustration as well as in stage art the Irish picturesque comprehended groupings of the human figure, it is not surprising that stage interiors were often carefully composed to achieve the same essential purpose as the exterior view. Domestic architecture was therefore related to the indigenous inhabitant with this end in mind. For Ireland, the cottage and the shebeen were regarded as sufficient representations of the picturesque domestic interior, and these two settings turn up repeatedly. The first scene of Grattan's *The White Boys* is *'the interior of an Irish shebeen . . . long table set out with pipes, jugs, glasses.'* Boucicault also utilized the picturesque interior, and as in his treatment of the landscape integrated it more closely with character and action. The third scene of *The Colleen Bawn* is the *'interior of* EILY's *cottage on Muckross Head – fire burning; table; armchair; stools; basin, sugar spoon, two jugs, tobacco, plate, knife, and lemon on table.'* Father Tom, peacefully smoking, is actually waiting for Myles to bring a jug of whiskey to make the punch; through the first part of the scene, which is concerned with the history of Eily's secret marriage to Hardress Cregan and Myles' love for her, runs a counterpointing and undercutting motif of drink quite characteristic of Boucicault's skilful blending of the comic with the serious, a motif naturally extended from the real domestic articles on the set to the expectations and character of Father Tom and Myles. The wedding celebrations of Arrah and Shaun the Post are more colourful, with beggars, children, a piper, fiddlers, and a crowd of wedding guests making a great deal of noise. Boucicault is also careful to allow his audience to see, through the open doors of the barn, the lights in the valley, and the abbey ruins and round tower beyond the village. In the scene at Eily's cottage the lake forms the background. Audiences must have found aesthetic pleasure in the artistic combination in the same scene of the interior picturesque and the landscape picturesque. Such a combination frequently occurs in Boucicault. His masterpiece of the interior picturesque is the wake scene in the last act of *The Shaughraun,* in which the supposedly murdered Conn is laid out in his mother's cabin: *'*CONN *is lying on a shutter,* L., *supported by an old table, a three-legged stool, and a keg. Table,* R., *covered with food and drinking cups, plates of snuff, jugs of punch, lighted candles in bottles, etc. Tableau of an Irish Wake.'* Peasants are seated around the room, and keeners sing a lament. Once again, it is worth pointing out that such a scene is not merely decorative, visually striking though it is. Conn is not dead at all, makes comic asides at the eulogies upon him, and surreptitiously swigs a handy jug of punch. The wake itself is directly related to his own character and the later dramatic action of the scene when the villain's henchmen nearly murder him a second time.

Boucicault's success in creating a more sophisticated type of Irish melodrama that mixed sensational incidents and effects with romantic landscape and plausible characterization was widely imitated in the 1860s, especially by Edward Falconer, who wrote a series of Irish dramas like *Peep O'Day, Killarney, Oonagh, Innisfallen,* and *Agra-ma-chree, or Gems of Ould Ireland.* This kind of drama was widely parodied: *The Colleen Bawn* instantly attracted burlesque, and H. J. Byron, the leading burlesque writer of his day, who had parodied Boucicault already, contributed *Green Grow the Rushes, Oh, or The Squireen, the Informer, and the Illicit Distiller,* a 'Hibernian sensation drama.' Other writers thought Boucicault's Ireland and Irishmen little improvement upon the older stage Ireland of comedy and farce. One of them was Shaw, who greatly admired Boucicault's stagecraft but accused him of 'blarneying the British public.' 'To an Irishman who has any sort of social conscience,' wrote Shaw, 'the conception of Ireland as a romantic picture in which the background is formed by the Lakes of Killarney by moonlight, and a round tower or so, whilst every male figure is "a broth of a bhoy", and every female one a colleen in a crimson Connemara cloak, is as exasperating as the conception of Italy as a huge garden and art museum, inhabited by picturesque artists' models, is to a sensible Italian.'[5] The fact that Shaw put his criticism·in pictorial and even picturesque terms demonstrates a complete understanding of Boucicault's visual technique, but it did not stop him from setting Act II of *John Bull's Other Island* in a landscape that would have done splendid theatrical service in the cause of the romantic sublime:

> *Westward a hillside of granite rock and heather slopes upward across the prospect from the south to the north. A huge stone stands on it in a naturally impossible place, as if it had been tossed up there by a giant. Over the brow, in the desolate valley beyond, is a round tower. A lonely white high road trending away westward past the tower loses itself at the foot of the far mountains. It is evening, and there are great breadths of silken green in the Irish sky. The sun is setting.*[6]

By 1896, when Shaw reviewed the revival of *The Colleen Bawn* that prompted his irritation with Boucicault and perhaps led him on to the satirical corrective of *John Bull's Other Island,* the vogue for Irish drama of this kind was nearly exhausted. On looking back over its history, one realizes how consistently it presented an Irish landscape simultaneously real and mythic, presented it according to long established modes of romantic composition, with the full and considerable ability of the scene-painter and stage carpenter. Boucicault's own part in the implementation of the pictorial aesthetic was an emphasis on a picturesque rather than a sublime Irish landscape, and closer links between this landscape, individualized character, and dramatic action than previous playwrights had achieved; yet he remained firmly in the same tradition. This, then, was the Irish landscape of the Victorian stage. What use later Irish dramatists made of it, how they absorbed it, and how they rejected it would be another subject in itself. One thing they could not do was ignore it.

NOTES

1 G. N. Wright, *Ireland Illustrated* (London, 1831), Preface.
2 N. P. Willis and J. Stirling Coyne, *The Scenery and Antiquities of Ireland* (London, 1846), I, iii.
3 *Ireland Illustrated,* Preface.
4 *Ibid.,* pp. 61, 65.
5 Bernard Shaw, *Our Theatres in the Nineties* (London, 1948 edition), II, 29.
6 Bernard Shaw, *John Bull's Other Island* (London, 1921), p. 29.

DOUBLE VISION IN ANGLO-IRISH LITERATURE

ANDREW CARPENTER

Any investigation into the influence of place on the personality of a group of writers must, of its nature, be speculative – and I am only too mindful of the scorn which has been heaped on those who admit to their work being 'speculative'. Swift, for instance, condemns one to the Academy of Lagado while the Irish scientist William Molyneux once referred to the speculative philosopher as a man merely 'unactive'.[1] But speculative or not, my subject is the personality of Irish, or rather Anglo-Irish writers and, through and beyond that, their way of looking at and coming to terms with life in Ireland: not only with the place and space around them, but also with their entire subject matter, in particular with themselves. There is, I think, a recognizable distinction between the Anglo-Irish writer and other writers, and this distinction is not so much bound up with differences of subject-matter, language, theme or even landscape as with a distinct difference in tone. Anglo-Irish literature has about it a particular atmosphere which distinguishes it clearly from English literature and often – though less often perhaps – from American literature too. The tone of Anglo-Irish writing is closely affected by the nature of the physical world of Ireland ('That ragged leaking raft held between sea and sea' as Richard Ryan describes it)[2] but tone is created by the writer himself and is a reflection of his personality rather than his subject matter. So instead of looking at the influence of particular places on particular Anglo-Irish writers, I want to explore some of the more general reasons why writing in Ireland seems to have developed a distinctive personality. I shall suggest that the reason is closely bound up with the way the writers look at things and that this is, in turn, conditioned by the facts of Irish history and the realities of social and cultural attitudes in Ireland.

Anglo-Irish writers seem, on the whole, to require of the reader a particular and rather sophisticated involvement. It is almost as if they are trying to justify or explore something beyond or through the looking-glass of the book in hand. There seems to be a central question which is always being suggested but seldom directly formulated or asked, and it is a question more connected with the writer than with his book. It is as if each book were an attempt at self-definition – not only books like *Ulysses* and *Gulliver's Travels* but also works like *Castle Rackrent* or *Langrishe Go Down*, much modern Irish poetry, some of Yeats, perhaps much of Synge. I find a constant and pervasive sense of authorial doubt and questioning in Anglo-Irish literature – a questioning which is far less noticeable elsewhere.

This sense of doubt and questioning – of uncertainty even – is most often resolved into a mode of writing which may broadly be called *ironic*. I am not suggesting that there is more surface irony – of statement, plot or situation – in Anglo-Irish writing than elsewhere; but there is an underlying irony of approach to the book as book, to writing as writing – an irony almost of conception – which seems to be peculiarly Irish. The works of Anglo-Irish writers spring often from a view of life that is continually probing the different values which exist in Ireland and testing them one against the other; they spring from an understanding of the fact that the intensity and colour of life in Ireland – and of the literature which reflects that life – comes at least in part from an enforced, continuous interrelationship between values, philosophies, languages and cultures antipathetic if not downright hostile to one another. Differing views exist actively side by side everywhere of course, but the passionate probing of their uneasy interaction is typical of much Anglo-Irish writing. An Englishman's book on Ireland may give the setting, the characters, the situation, a good idea of place and space; but does it not, nearly always, lack the peculiar tension of a book which springs from the Irish consciousness?

My point may become clear if we compare David Thomson's *Woodbrook* (1974) with Tom Kilroy's *The Big Chapel* (1971). Kilroy's book, which we classify as Anglo-Irish, seems fascinated with the exploration of uncertainty, not only within the novel but outside it as well. It is an exploration of the tensions of the Irish character, the author's own as much as those of the characters in the book, while David Thomson's book is a *description* of himself in Ireland. There is a kind of peaceful acceptance of things Irish in Thomson's book – a passionate probing of them in Kilroy's. Furthermore, where the reader of David Thomson's book can relax and let the book flow over him, the reader of Tom Kilroy's book must stay utterly alert; he is being involved in the process of the book in a crucial way. This active involvement of the reader in the process of testing and judging the values proposed in the book is part, I think, of the personality of Anglo-Irish writing and of the fascination which it exerts over us. The tensions aroused in this process of active reading are best described – *faute de mieux*, I am afraid – as broadly akin to those of irony. For various things are being assessed and weighed against each other at different levels of one's experience, and at the same time here, (just as they are in the simpler forms of irony), and the tensions they create rubbing against each other are the life of the book and of the process of its reading.

Irony, in any of its manifestations, is more difficult to come to grips with than the other elements of a work of literature. In the first place, to *explain* irony is almost by definition to destroy its effect since the pleasure of irony rests to a large extent on the pretence that the intelligent reader has seen, with the writer, the real truth which is hidden from others. The pleasure is, of course, that one sees two things at once, and after assessing both, decides which is the surface truth and which the real truth. A further development of this is an effect of double perspective not necessarily intended by the author; here the reader can see two authorial perspectives in action; he does not judge between them, but allows each to throw light on the other. Seamus Heaney, Tom Kinsella and John Montague are the Irishmen of their landscapes, in their landscapes; yet they are also commenting on their landscapes – on the place and situation of Ireland – as if they were outside the books as well as in them. (Joyce can do this as well of course: and Yeats does it in 'Among School Children'.) It is as if the writers see themselves double: Heaney in the woods escaping the massacre, Kinsella following the route of the Táin, Montague bumping down to Tyrone in the bus: yet each, as well, is active outside the poem, defining, explaining, analysing with the reader the relationship between the poet and the person who bears his name in the poem, as well as the effect of place upon

175

that person. The whole exercise seems to be aimed at clarification of both Heaneys, Kinsellas or Montagues, so that each may be freed from what is obviously a personal, but may well be also a cultural sense of insecurity. As Montague puts it: 'One explores an inheritance to free oneself and others.'[3] The process of being read, and the process of writing are parts of the process of self-discovery and definition; thus a work such as *The Rough Field* incorporates the author's questionings and indeed the author himself in the constantly shifting perspectives and in the commentary which runs through the work. This commenting on itself is, as Hugh Kenner has pointed out, a step towards deliberate discontinuity and it becomes, in both Swift and Joyce, a fundamental gadget in the complicated games of ventriloquy which confront the reader. In Montague though, the aim is to manipulate the different perspectives and so allow a definition of self to emerge from the poem by implication – in *The Rough Field* a definition linked loosely but crucially to place. Many other modern Anglo-Irish poets are doing the same sort of thing in their poems of landscape: Heaney, Kinsella, Derek Mahon, Richard Murphy and others. What seems to be a definition of landscape turns out to be a highly sophisticated definition of self, seen from outside the poem as well as from within. Here is another example:

> . . . through a forest,
> by a salt-dark shore,
> by a standing stone on a dark plain,
> by a ford running blood,
> and along this gloomy pass, with someone ahead
> calling and waving on the crest, against a heaven
> of dismantling cloud – transfixed
> by the same figure (stopped, pointing)
> on the rampart at Cruachan
> where it began . . .
> the morning sunlight pouring on us all
> as we scattered over the mounds
> disputing over useless old books,
> assembled in cheerful speculation
> around a prone block, *Miosgán Medba,*
> – Queen Medb's *turd* . . .? – and rattled our maps,
> joking together in growing illness

or age or fat; before us
the route of the Táin, over men's dust,
toward these hills that seemed to grow
darker as we drove nearer.[4]

The tone of a poem like this – Kinsella's 'The Route of the Táin' – is probably its greatest strength: sophisticated, passionate, searching – the author ironic in the wings – it seems natural and expected until one turns to other contemporary poetry being written outside Ireland and fails to find anything like it. Perhaps some modern American poetry tends towards it, but it is certainly not to be found in English poetry. There are poems of self-definition in modern English poetry – in Jon Stallworthy and Philip Larkin to name but two – and yet their tone is much less passionate and searching, their perspectives less shifting, their point of view so much more settled. Perhaps it would be too fanciful to suggest that English poets have an inbuilt cultural, linguistic, social and historical security which makes, say, 'The Whitsun Weddings' a much slighter, less demanding poem than Derek Mahon's poem about the disused shed in Co. Wexford, or *The Rough Field* or 'The Route of the Táin'. The Anglo-Irish writer from Swift to Hugh Maxton seems to revel in the exploration of and sometimes the triumphant defence of a personal lack of security; his insecurity is, if you like, his roots. Larkin's insecurity is an individual problem which certainly could, and possibly should, be psycho-analysed and, in the end, cured. Heaney, Montague and Kinsella will never be cured – nor indeed want to be cured: they must seek out more places, images, words and sounds to restate the belief that the insecurity they celebrate is insoluble.

At its simplest level, of course, the insecurity is a linguistic and cultural one. No one writing in Ireland – not even Daniel Corkery, Frank O'Connor or Robert Farren – is both wholly Gaelic Irish and wholly inside the English language. The compromise each writer makes as he writes of Ireland in English, is almost a racial one. Beckett, by retreating into French and translating back into English, is the only one to solve this problem satisfactorily, though it obviously bothers many contemporary Anglo-Irish poets since they spend so much time translating from the Irish language. Yeats, with magnificent arrogance, faced the problem of compromise by shooting it down and creating a

177

mythic tradition of eighteenth-century Anglo-Irish writers in whose conservative, non-mercantile footsteps he could – like a latter-day page to Berkeley's King Wenceslaus – tread with security. But he too came to a form of compromise in his remarks on the influence of Davis, Mangan and Ferguson.[5] For Synge, the compromise hurt most when the subject-matter he was drawn to was attached to writing he could not, in his maturity, admire. He put it like this in his autobiography:

> The Irish ballad poetry of 'The Spirit of the Nation' school engrossed me for a while and made [me] commit my most serious literary error; I thought it excellent for a considerable time and then repented bitterly.[6]

Later, of course, he squared his debt to Irish language and culture in *The Aran Islands* where, in Book IV, he himself provided translations of Irish poems which the shanachie described as 'much finer things than his old bits of rhyme.'[7]

To some extent, this awareness of two living cultures – the writer not feeling he belongs properly to either – accounts at the most obvious level for the Anglo-Irish writer's insecurity and his need to take up a position of ironic detachment from his creation: but this is only part of the reason.

Far more important, I think, in the conditions which have given rise to the writer's attitude, are the double visions and double interpretations forced upon him by the facts of Irish history and of everyday life in Ireland. There have always – certainly since the reign of Queen Elizabeth I – been two distinct ways of looking at and interpreting many things in Ireland – place, person or event – both of which have credibility and both of which must often be taken into account at one and the same time. Growing into an awareness of this fundamental fact of Irish life is, I think, one of the main themes of Joyce's *A Portrait of the Artist*. There are, Stephen learns, two distinct ways of looking at the figure of Parnell: each view is respectable, each knows it is right; and yet each must take grudging but positive account of the existence of the other view. Only after a process of linguistic and social self-definition can anyone born or bred in Ireland develop the confidence to react to the dualities of Irish life; like many another Irish artist, Stephen reacts at the end of the novel by adopting a studied, aggressive tone of ironic detachment.

The problem is that so much in Ireland can validly be interpreted in two ways. The stately Georgian architecture of Dublin, for instance, can be seen as a useless relic of hated oppression, or as the finest example of Irish craftsmanship in the eighteenth century. The Irish language may be seen as a pointless anachronism or as the key to national identity. Everyone brought up in Ireland is very soon made aware of multiple points of view on many things, and one learns also that opposing points of view are often both quite respectable, and that they can be made to sound so. It is even – ironic though this may seem to an outsider – respectable to follow the Republican tradition to the extent of supporting those who wish to subvert the establishment: but it is also, of course, respectable to support the establishment. This situation has existed, in various forms, for three hundred years.

The idea that opposing views are, in a sense, equally acceptable, is wittily exploited by Synge at the end of *The Shadow of the Glen.* The choice between the world of the tramp and the world of the settled community does not really have to be made, for they may co-exist. Yet if a member of the audience does want to opt for Dan Burke or for the tramp, he makes his decision for reasons that he brings from outside the play: Synge has not provided a right or a wrong within the play. The ending of the action is deliberately ambiguous, and it is the reader's own personality which determines his attitude towards the worlds of the characters. Similarly at the end of *The Playboy of the Western World,* the two cultures, of the playboy and of the settled fools of Mayo, are seen to take up a simultaneous existence. The playboy goes out romping, and Pegeen will settle herself by the fire. It is a sophisticated solution to the old problem of the distinction between the comic and the tragic in literature, and Synge must have realized this when he described the play as an extravaganza: for it is simultaneously comic and tragic – enigmatically so – and leaves our minds working over the events and characters of the play, since it has forced on us neither a romantic ending nor a death. (Shaw and Wilde both tend towards this type of effect as well.) One's response to a play such as *The Playboy* must be personal and to some extent at least, self-revelatory. The play

179

cannot really be said to have a meaning or a message unless individual members of an audience or individual readers choose to put it there. The play itself, in fact, aims not at providing answers but at exploring and highlighting the tensions between different views or perspectives on life; it leaves one with an appreciation of the fact that apparently contradictory things can exist simultaneously and, in fact in the order of life as it is, must do so. Here as elsewhere, the aspirations of the Anglo-Irish writer in his work are not single or simple; they are excitingly various, and it is the sense of one's involvement in this variety, through the different perceptions, that is at the heart of the work's fascination.

Another exploitation of double vision can be seen in several of the recent novels about the big house. In many cases, the relationship explored is between the offspring of the landlord – a weak son or a spinster daughter who symbolises genuine if faded gentility, since he or she plays the piano, or gardens, or is a connoisseur of wine – and a tenant, crude, and from a priest-ridden background, yet full of the vigour and life-force which the other lacks. The sympathies of the writer and of the reader are divided – and genuinely so. The two sides of the relationship can never be brought wholly together, and yet one feels for both, and is torn and puzzled to see them irreconcilable. Again there are two worlds which one must see simultaneously, and any choice between them is a choice made more for personal reasons which the reader brings with him from outside the book, than for reasons in the book. The process of reading involves the reader very fully once again and the writer, standing back in the wings, is faced with the same problems of weighing and comparing the different perspectives as is the reader. For such a writer, to write about life in Ireland is to reflect the ambiguities and tensions of life defined in double standards, double judgements and double visions.

If, as I am maintaining, the excitement and tension of Anglo-Irish literature is the result of a need to see life in Ireland in a different way from the way one would see life elsewhere, then we should perhaps spend a moment on the physical aspects of double vision. The mechanics and philosophy of visual perception were, of course, very much the concern of the experimental philosophers of the seventeenth and eighteenth centuries, including those in Ireland. A generation before Berkeley's important *Essay towards a New Theory of Vision* (1709), William Molyneux, a leading light of that fascinating group of inspired eccentrics, the Dublin Philosophical Society, confronted the problem of double vision in the physical sense in his *Dioptrica Nova* (1692). In a chapter entitled 'An Optick Problem of Double Vision' he tries to explain how it is that, though we have two eyes, we do not see everything double all the time.

> . . . I assert first, that we do see all objects in two places, . . . [but] the Mind or visive faculty takes no notice that there are two *Axes Optici,* or two Pictures made by those *Axes Optici* on each *Retina,* but following back, and hunting *counter* alongst these *Axes,* it is directed to, and determined in one single Point, and therefore sees it as *one.* . . . From hence this Paradoxical Corollary arises: *That an Object may be seen in two places, and yet not seen double.*[8]

Molyneux contends that we see everything we look at through two different perspectives – one from each eye – but that the mind constantly corrects the doubleness and gives us a single image. It is the doubleness of our vision – whether corrected by the mind or not – which gives depth to our visive faculty, and it is a similar doubleness of vision in the perception of the Anglo-Irish writer, I maintain (often deliberately left uncorrected or deliberately exploited), which gives a particular type of depth to his work.

It is a function of Molyneux's 'Paradoxical Corollary' that certain events in Irish history have double – and mutually exclusive – descriptive terms: Easter Rising and Easter Rebellion; Patriot Parliament and Jacobite Parliament; and certain terms have double interpretations: loyalist, big house, patriot, perhaps even the word 'border'. One must be aware of these double perspectives and aware of them simultaneously: thus, as some northern poets have found, the foundations of any literary structure, secure from one point of view, are likely to be insecure from another. One man's rock foundation is another man's sand: one man's compromise is another man's surrender: one man's Holy Father is another man's Anti-Christ: one man's Coole Park or Lissadell is to another man a symbol of hated oppression. And

181

each interpretation is, in its way, valid. This surely explains why, in Anglo-Irish literature at any rate, one is so often being forced to test oneself, to clarify and amend one's view of the world, as one acts out the part of 'reader'.

It is interesting that we find this need for at least an acknowledgement of the other way of seeing things even in the Penal Laws of the eighteenth century – where one would least expect it. The wording of a law of 1695 declaring which days in the year shall be observed as holy days seems straightforward and provocative enough on first reading.

Whereas many idle persons refuse to work at their lawful calling and labour on several days in the year, on pretence that the same is dedicated to some saint or pretended saint, patron or pretended patron, for whom they have or pretend to have reverence or respect, and chuse rather to spend such days in idleness, drunkenness and vice, to the scandal of religion, . . . every such person so refusing . . . being convicted . . . shall forfeit the sum of two shillings; and if such offender shall neglect or refuse to pay the said sum, he shall be publickly whipped within 24 hours after such order be made.[9]

But in the next paragraph, the lawmakers go on to set out in detail the punishments to be inflicted on those justices who refuse to convict under this law and those constables who refuse to put the law into effect or to whip offenders. In other words, the law acknowledges that it is merely one way of looking at life and seems to accept that the other perspective is *de facto* to remain in existence. Again, there is the notorious law of 1692 which declares that Protestant maidens and women who take to husband papists or popish persons, ('to the great Dishonour of Almighty God,') shall be deemed dead in law. Dead by one eye, and alive by another. And obviously the official eye often winked, for there are prohibitions against *too much conniving* at the existence of papist schools: not against conniving at them at all, but against too much conniving.

Through the philosophy behind these acts runs a perception of doubles; two religions in action, two cultures in action, two philosophies. Though the law appears to demand adherence to the one code, it acknowledges the power and existence of the other.

The lawmakers could see two things at once and yet persuade themselves that they were not seeing double.

The world in which one sees two things at once becomes merely confusing, in life as in literature, without rigorous technical control. The oculist controls the physical phenomenon of double vision by means of different lenses for the different eyes and so tries to eliminate the confusion. The writer, wanting often to exploit the doubleness, must act with more circumspection. He is, after all, trying to clarify an object by deliberately distorting it first one way and then another so that when the reader finally corrects the perspective for himself, he sees the object far more carefully and attentively than he would otherwise have done. The writer's aim is to put forward a distorted perspective as if it were the only one, but to do so in terms which will make the intelligent reader aware of another perspective, and so able to see the two together and judge the object clearly because he is aware of the earlier distortion. But the tone of the original false perspective must be cool and convincing enough for it to be *just* possible for a mistake to be made. Take the most famous example of this technique:

> A Modest Proposal for preventing the children of poor people in *Ireland* from being a burthen to their parents or country, and for making them beneficial to the public.[10]

The tone of this work, from the archness of its title to the final ingenuous statement that since the proposer's wife is past child-bearing, he can not be accused of trying to make any money out of fattening his own children for slaughter, is so carefully controlled that it is just possible that there could, somewhere, be a reader so one-eyed that he would really take the proposal seriously. Yet all the rest of us, because we are reasonably human, are immediately aware of the distortion of perspective; so we automatically keep our other eye – our moral eye – particularly carefully alert to compensate for the distortion of the modest proposer's eye. Thus we see the suffering poor of Ireland in a double perspective which greatly clarifies the vision we would have received from yet another serious pamphlet on the need for granaries or poor laws in Ireland in 1729. Swift's technique, by its

183

very coolness and control, succeeds in arousing in us a truly *saeva indignatio.*

In a sense, much of the cool, controlled poetry of modern Anglo-Irish writing makes the same type of demand on its readers – though the intensity of the response is, of course, rather less – as does Swift's pamphlet. Writers in Ireland, like the rest of us in Ireland, do still see the world double, and find the vision alarmingly unsettling. When they come to write about life in Ireland, their viewpoints shift and slide, their perspectives alter; there is seldom, in Anglo-Irish writing, a definite viewpoint or a certain right or wrong – are there, incidentally, many Irish detective stories? – nor is there an omniscient narrator or what one might call a normative perspective. Far more often, the writer is concerned with an ambiguous consciousness and its relationship with the reader; and within that consciousness – Thady or Gulliver or the Modest Proposer or Leopold Bloom or even Crazy Jane – are at least two simultaneous perceptions: traditional values and mercantile values, Protestant rights and Catholic rights, heroism and the settled world, the massacred and the perpetrator of the massacre, a world with God and a world without God, the old man and the dancers. What is important is that all these sets of visions are co-existent; after all, the tension between appearance and reality is at the heart of many works of literature in many cultures; but the simultaneous awareness of two appearances and two realities is, I am inclined to think, an important element in the tone of Anglo-Irish writing and the personality of the Anglo-Irish writer.

Perhaps my point could be clarified by the application of these guidelines to some simple examples. In common with many thinkers of the seventeenth and eighteenth centuries, Swift and Pope were interested in providing a definition of man. *Gulliver's Travels* and 'An Essay on Man' are both, in my view, designed to provide such a definition. The actual definitions, when they come, are not very different from each other, but the means which the authors choose to reach their goals could hardly be further apart. Pope's 'Essay on Man' is a poem of statement, of logical argument, presenting a positive, formal position.

> Know then thyself, presume not God to scan;
> The proper study of Mankind is Man.

Plac'd on this isthmus of a middle state,
A being darkly wise, and rudely great:
With too much knowledge for the Sceptic side,
With too much weakness for the Stoic's pride,
He hangs between; in doubt to act, or rest,
In doubt to deem himself a God, or Beast;
In doubt his Mind or Body to prefer,
Born but to die, and reas'ning but to err; . . .
Created half to rise, and half to fall;
Great lord of all things, yet a prey to all;
Sole judge of Truth, in endless Error hurl'd:
The glory, jest, and riddle of the world! [11]

In *Gulliver's Travels* Swift, instead of stating that man has 'too much knowledge for the Sceptic side,' or 'too much weakness for the Stoic's pride,' or is 'in doubt to deem himself a God, or Beast; In doubt his Mind or Body to prefer,' shows us man's excesses through the simple device of double perspectives, and allows the definition to emerge, in the mind of the reader, by negatives. The Gulliver figure (who, you will remember, suffers from short sight and is constantly worried about whether his glasses are safe) is forced to see himself time and again in terms of gross visual distortion. Yet Swift's art makes this gullible narrator's perspective so persuasive that the reader himself forgets to keep his other eye open; at the end of the fourth book, the reader is about to agree with Gulliver that, yes it is a good idea to sleep in a stable and desert one's wife and yes, horses do smell far nicer than humans, when he must – at least one hopes that he must – wake up and see that a hideous joke has been played on his gullible perceptions. His response must be an active one as he realizes that man is not really as he has been led by Gulliver to see him: man is not as filthy as a Yahoo, nor as coldly rational as a Houyunhnm, nor as ridiculously benevolent as a Brobdingnagian, nor as speculative as a Laputan nor as politically small-minded as a Lilliputian, and so on. In fact a positive message emerges by implication, and the message is seen to be the same as Pope's: that man is 'the glory, jest and riddle of the world.' Swift has shown the reader all the things that man is not, and shown them so persuasively by means of visual distortions, that the reader reacts against what he sees. Thus Swift's positive, an emotional, physical

185

and intellectual compromise, emerges not in the pages of the book, but in the mind of the reader. The use of different perspectives here is extremely sophisticated, of course, and the reader must be aware that Gulliver's own perspective is constantly shifting too: but the book's working is, I think, essentially bound up with the mechanics of double, simultaneous vision in the way that Pope's is not. *Gulliver's Travels* operates outrageously on the reader's sensibilities because it demands simultaneous, double interpretation: one eye of the mind, as it were, delightedly accepts the world of Lilliput as logical and even, possibly, credible until we come to Gulliver's frantic denials that he has ever had improper relations with the wife of Flimnap, the Lord High Treasurer, – an excellent lady, but only six inches tall. The other eye of the mind puts things into the correct perspective and the reader, one hopes, laughs – amused partly at his own gullibility since he had so nearly been duped into seeing with one eye only. The fact that the reader has, normally in life as in literature, a sense of double, simultaneous, deep vision is crucial to the working of the passage, as the distorted perspective of the first eye's vision only becomes apparent when the second eye gets to work. The reader of 'An Essay on Man' may well see with a single eye only and still gain the full and correct perspective of the argument since it is operating 'straight', as it were, and directly on the mind.

Another example of this distinction between methods can be found in the works of Maria Edgeworth and Jane Austen. It is a truism to say that Jane Austen's work is founded on an ironic vision of life, but the irony of, say, *Persuasion,* complicated though it is, is an irony of techniques and of surface rather than an irony which springs from the author's conception of the book itself. Despite the various levels of meaning we experience in reading *Persuasion,* there is here – as elsewhere in Jane Austen's work – what one could call a normative perspective: that is, the reader knows what should be the correct response to Sir Walter Elliot, or Anne, or Captain Wentworth or Mary. He knows because Jane Austen constantly gives him the sense of being not only in control of the novel, but also in control of his responses to it; in fact, she frequently tells him precisely how he should react. The adjectives she uses to describe her characters are often adjectives which imply a judgement, and she goes further than·

this. For instance, after the splendid opening paragraphs of the novel in which Sir Walter is seen reading his own entry in the Baronetage, Jane Austen does not leave the reader to work out what this would seem to indicate of his character: she spells it out with devastating clarity: 'Vanity was the beginning and the end of Sir Walter Elliot's character.' We enjoy the irony of her description, but we see that we have not been allowed to share in any process of testing the impression we have received against our own sensibilities; we are not, ourselves, to be tested, not to be allowed through the looking glass of the book we hold in our hands. To say this is not in any way to derogate from Jane Austen's skill: she is playing a particular game with her characters and the reader is not very crucially involved in it. After all the story of *Persuasion* is to be, at heart, a straight romance in which the heroine finally gets her man.

But when we turn from *Persuasion* to *Castle Rackrent,* we see at once that we are to be a part of the game, and that it is a very different game. The irony we encounter here is not merely that of technique or of surface – though both are certainly present – but an irony that underlies the very conception of this book. From the first page, the reader hardly knows how seriously he should be taking the book in front of him, or its narrator, or its story or its author – if indeed it has an author: for the fiction that Maria Edgeworth is merely the editor of the memoirs which make up the book is maintained fairly consistently throughout. At the centre of the book's unreliability is the figure of the narrator, Thady, who must pose – and is certainly intended to pose – a serious problem for the serious reader. But even if we accept Maria Edgeworth's terms sufficiently to accept Thady as the narrator of the story, there is still precious little in the novel that we can relate to the realities of life as we know it on our side of the looking glass: from the name 'Rackrent' to the impossibility of so much of the action, we suspect – whether we are 'serious' readers or not – that we are being continually teased and tested. There seems to be very little that is 'straight' about the book, and very little that encourages us to trust the author. The characters are constantly shifting towards caricature, and any serious values which are introduced tend to dissolve into pathos or farce. Thady's relationship with the reader is one of ironic detachment some of the time, and of downright deception at

187

other times. Yet we do not merely throw the book down in exasperation: we find that we have been, in a subtle way, involved in its process. For the reader's reaction to Thady and his story is not determined by Maria Edgeworth, but by his own beliefs and prejudices – how he has been taught Irish history, his attitude to landlordism or to the mercantile values of Thady's son, Jason. Thus the reader's own views form an essential part of the process of reading *Castle Rackrent*. It is interesting that Irish students, many of whom have somehow imbibed the view that all landlords in eighteenth-century Ireland were villains, are inclined to treat Thady as a reliable narrator and the book itself as a useful social document, while English students are inclined – in my experience – to dismiss it as so much Irish Cock and Bull. I would maintain that such divergencies prove the success of Maria Edgeworth's technique and show that the book's excitement lies in the way it uses the reader, forcing him to take account of different viewpoints and perspectives – to respond. As a result of his experience of the book, the reader finds himself drawn into the perennial problems of Ireland and Irish society. But Maria Edgeworth is not making statements herself about these problems so much as pushing them towards the reader through the characters and actions in the book. It is the reader, in the end, whose view of the world is broadened and deepened by his response to the positives and negatives of the various ways of life shown in the novel; the richness of the novel's experience springs from the double, or even treble, perspectives which the author presents to the reader's gaze.

In the end, I suppose, the reasons for the differences between these examples are very simple: history, culture and temperament. Life in Ireland has always – well, certainly since the Battle of the Boyne – been a more enigmatic and ambiguous affair than life in England and Anglo-Irish writers, those of today no less than those of past generations, do no more than reflect this element of enigma and ambiguity in the way they conceive of their subjects and their characters, and in the relationship they develop with their readers. But I would maintain that the personality of Irish writing (if such a thing can really be said to exist), lies in a persistent and continuing interest in the plurality of Irish attitudes and the uncertainties of Irish life. Even where the writer is not specifically aiming to exploit these uncertainties, the very ambiguities of life around him are likely to influence the tone of what he writes.

Whether he is aware of it or not then, I suggest that the Anglo-Irish writer sees and interprets the world through the perspective of continuous, simultaneous and inescapable double or multiple vision. It is this which helps to give his work the depth, richness and mystery which, so often, are its distinguishing characteristics, and which make it, for the reader, an almost continual challenge.

NOTES

1 William Molyneux, *Sciothericum Telescopicum* (Dublin, 1686), Epistle Dedicatory.
2 Richard Ryan, *Ravenswood* (Dublin, 1973), p. 37.
3 John Montague, *The Rough Field* (Dublin, 1972 ed.), back cover.
4 Thomas Kinsella, 'The Route of the Táin', *New Poems 1973* (Dublin, 1973), p. 58.
5 See *Davis, Mangan, Ferguson? Tradition and the Irish Writer: Writings by W. B. Yeats and by Thomas Kinsella* (Dublin, 1970), pp. 15-53.
6 *J. M. Synge: Collected Works* (London, 1962-8), II, 13.
7 *Ibid.*, 172.
8 William Molyneux, *Dioptrica Nova* (London, 1692), pp. 290, 293.
9 *Statutes at Large (Ireland)*, (Dublin, 1786), 7 William III, Chapter XIV.
10 *The Prose Writings of Jonathan Swift*, ed. Herbert Davis (Oxford, 1939-68), XII.
11 *Pope: Poetical Works*, ed. Herbert Davis (London, O.U.P., 1966), p. 250.

CONTRIBUTORS

A. NORMAN JEFFARES, a Dubliner with Wexford ancestry, has taught in the universities of Dublin, Groningen, Edinburgh, Adelaide, Leeds and Stirling, where he is now Professor of English Studies. He has written books and articles on various Anglo-Irish writers, as well as editing their work. He has also published work in Restoration and eighteenth-century English literature, and in American and Commonwealth literature.

ROBERT O'DRISCOLL, Professor of English at St. Michael's College, University of Toronto, comes from Newfoundland and studied at Memorial University and the University of London. He was the founder and first chairman of the Canadian Association for Irish Studies, and founder and artistic director of the Irish Theatre Society and the Irish Arts Theatre in Toronto. He is the author of books on Yeats and Samuel Ferguson and is joint general editor of the *Yeats Studies* series, of which four volumes have been published.

F. S. L. LYONS, a former Fellow and now Provost of Trinity College, Dublin, has been writing about Irish history for nearly thirty years. He is the author of several books, three of which – *The Irish Parliamentary Party, The Fall of Parnell* and *John Dillon* – are concerned with the Parnellite period. His biography, *Charles Stewart Parnell*, appeared in the spring of 1977, and he is now at work on the authorised life of W. B. Yeats.

ANN SADDLEMYER, Professor of English at Victoria College and Director of the Graduate Centre for Study of Drama at the University of Toronto, is a Canadian by birth. She has published books and articles on the works of W. B. Yeats, J. M. Synge, Lady Gregory, and other modern dramatists, and served as chairman of the International Association for the Study of Anglo-Irish Literature from 1973-76.

Contributors

RICHARD WALL holds a Ph.D. from the National University of Ireland and is Associate Professor and Assistant Head of the English Department of the University of Calgary, Alberta. He has published articles and reviews on Joyce and Behan in *Ariel, James Joyce Quarterly* and *Modern Drama.*

BRIAN COFFEY, who was a student at University College, Dublin with Denis Devlin, has been writing and publishing poetry since the 1930s. He edited the poems of Denis Devlin and also Devlin's *The Heavenly Foreigner.* His latest book, *The Big Laugh,* was published during the IASAIL conference in Galway.

MICHAEL R. BOOTH is the foundation Professor of Theatre Studies at the University of Warwick. He taught formerly at the University of British Columbia, the Royal Military College of Canada, and the University of Guelph, Ontario. His publications include *English Melodrama* and three editions: *Eighteenth Century Tragedy, Hiss the Villain* (a selection of melodrama), and the five-volume *English Plays of the Nineteenth Century.*

ANDREW CARPENTER is a College Lecturer in the Department of Modern English and American Literature at University College, Dublin. His publications include articles and books on Anglo-Irish literature of the eighteenth century and an edition of E. M. Stephens's life of his uncle J. M. Synge, *My Uncle John* (Oxford University Press, 1974).

LORNA REYNOLDS, Professor of English at University College, Galway, has written extensively on many aspects of Anglo-Irish literature. She is joint editor of the *Yeats Studies* series.

INDEX

193

195